MW01006419

OUTSMART
YOUR BRAIN

SECOND EDITION

Dr. Marcia Reynolds

How to Master Your Mind When Emotions Take the Wheel

Published by: Covisioning
www.outsmartyourbrain.com

Copyright © 2017 by Marcia Reynolds

All rights reserved. No part of this book may be reproduced or transmitted in any form whatsoever, electronic or mechanical, without written permission from Covisioning, except for brief quotations attributed to Marcia Reynolds embodied in articles or reviews.

Published by:
Covisioning
1601 E. Echo Lane
Phoenix, AZ 85020
602-954-9030
marcia@outsmartyourbrain.com

Second edition
ISBN: 978-0-9655250-7-7 (print)
       978-0-9655250-3-9 (eBook)

Editor: Natasha Hunter

Book design: 1106 Design

Back cover photo: Tina Celle

Printed in the United States of America

How to order:
Copies may be ordered from Covisioning.
Quantity discount available by calling 602-954-9030.

Visit us at *www.outsmartyourbrain.com* for updates and articles.

"When I dare to act in the service of my vision, it is no longer important that which I am afraid."
—**Audre Lorde,**
Activist and Philosopher

"They want you to be present more than they need you to be perfect."
—**Marcia Reynolds,**
from The Discomfort Zone: How Leaders Turn Difficult Conversations into Breakthroughs

TABLE OF CONTENTS

AN INTRODUCTION
TO TRAINING YOUR BRAIN

When Self-Talk Doesn't Work

I was watching a talk show where a famous relationship expert was coaching a woman onstage. She admitted taunting her husband during fights, picking at him where he was most vulnerable. She knew this wasn't fighting fairly but she couldn't stop. The expert said, "Yes you can. Just stop." The woman sat down a bit bewildered and totally embarrassed. I knew her problem would persist.

For years, "Change your thoughts, you change your behavior" was the mantra for life improvement. Through experience and science, we have since learned that affirmations rarely change behavior when emotions have taken the wheel. When your buttons get pushed into anger and your mind floods with fear, telling yourself to be calm or courageous won't stand up to the voices in your head telling you to defend or shut up.

In the end, the "Just do it" mantra has created more guilt than success. People wonder why they are so weak they just can't do it—change their diet, speak up to their boss, ask their spouse to be more supportive—and spend most of their days feeling angry or resign themselves to living thick-skinned lives.

Why is making the best choices for yourself so hard? **You are under the spell of your emotions.** When emotions take over, logic disappears.

For years, I taught principles of self-talk, then called myself a fraud when I'd take my anger out on my partner or turn down an opportunity because I was afraid of looking stupid. Even when I tried meditating and visualizing white lights around irritating people, there were few days where my emotions weren't triggered to a point of no return.

Then I discovered Daniel Goleman's book, **Emotional Intelligence.** As I dug into the research, I discovered there was a Wizard of Oz controlling my mind behind the curtains. By applying Goleman's theories to my own work using coaching skills, cognitive psychology, conflict resolution, and sensory awareness, I found I could pull back the curtains and take control of my reactions. The emotions didn't go away; I just learned ways I could recognize when they appeared in my body, understand the reason for their existence, and then shift my emotional state before they overpowered my consciousness. I could then choose my reactions for myself. I learned how to create a mind of my own.

I now present workshops globally on Reflective Intelligence, Using Emotional Intelligence in the Workplace, and Emotional Engagement for Leaders where I teach others how to keep their brains from sabotaging their desires. The participants learn how to shift their emotional states to make better choices for themselves. Those who are most resistant—who shudder at the thought of discussing feelings—generally become my greatest champions by the end of the class. The reason? They experience what it feels like to be free of the tyranny of their brains.

If you don't pay attention to and deal with your emotions, they will hold you in contempt, undermining your perspective, your decision-making, your relationships, and your happiness. If instead you learn how to read the emotional states that naturally occur in your bodies, you are better able to connect with others, cope with daily stressors, and feel more peace and joy on your life.

Humans are Emotional, and Employees are Humans

"The most important need for leaders today…" my ears perked up. The well-known speaker was addressing an audience of HR professionals. He had presented some diagrams showing the abysmal state of employee engagement, numbers I had sadly been sharing for years. I was hoping for a brilliant insight when he said, "…is to hold one-on-one conversations with their employees." Wasn't this the message I was asked to deliver when I taught my first management training class over thirty years ago?

I believe leaders prefer to manage resources instead of people because dealing with humans is unpredictable and messy. Humans are emotional by nature, even those who claim they only act with logic and sensibility. Everything seen, heard, felt, touched, and smelled is processed through two emotional centers in the brain before the logical center is accessed.

Emotions aren't bad; they are reactions to stimuli. They reflect energy moving through the body. For both the person who has feelings and the leader hoping to have a meaningful conversation, acknowledging instead of ignoring the emotions in the moment can lead to discovering important information needed to break through blocks, make good decisions, and take a positive step forward.

Emotions have far more impact on our relationships than our words. What you feel will determine if people feel safe enough to open to you. Even if they trust you to be honest with them, they need to feel it is okay to be themselves and say what is on their mind without worrying about being negatively judged.

If you weren't raised to talk about emotions, you don't know how to respond to them when they show up. You hide or rationalize your own feelings and then negate, shut down, or tune out when others slip and reveal how they feel.

Many leaders have said to me, "If I encourage people to talk about their feelings, I'm afraid their emotions will make me do things I wouldn't normally do." Or, "I don't have time for their dramas." The business world is full of aphorisms that declare, "Only the tough survive."

Being uncomfortable with expressions of emotions doesn't make you bad. Your discomfort is an indication that you haven't had enough training to develop your skills. When you learn how to use the power of sensory awareness—to feel deeply and empathize with others—you will connect more effectively with others and your conversations will have a more powerful impact.

Understanding how emotions affect decisions and behavior makes you wise. Giving people the safe space to talk about their emotions makes you strong. The leader who develops the skills of reflective intelligence so they are aware of their reactions and choices, and then emotional intelligence to better interact with others, will feel more confident and empowered. Their relationships will improve and they will comfortably increase engagement, innovation, and results.

I know this is easier said than done. Staying alert to your feelings and encouraging others to express themselves can be scary and even painful. That's why I wrote this book. First, the book will help you understand why you do what you do so you can make the best choices for yourself. Then you will be given tools and techniques for developing the courage and sensitivity you need to have meaningful one-on-one conversations with others.

When the Full Human Being Shows Up

My first job out of college was in the training department for a group of psychiatric hospitals. During my second year, we had a big layoff. I witnessed an amazing event the day after.

Every department head, from maintenance, to aides, to the nursing staff, brought the people that worked for them together to sit in a circle in an empty room. One at a time, each person in the circle declared how he or she felt. "I'm angry they didn't find a better way to fix the problem." "I'm scared about when the next shoe will drop." "I'm sad because my best friend lost her job."

The leaders didn't try to fix the people or promise things would get better. Each leader accepted what was shared, and then said things like, "I understand why you feel that way," or "It makes sense that you think the actions were untimely or wrong." After every person expressed his or herself, the leader said, "Thank you. I hope we can continue to support each other through this time. Do you think we can talk about moving forward now or would you prefer we wait a day or two?" The group then decided what they would do next.

I worked for three companies after that one. Then I started my own business and have worked with leaders in thirty-six countries. I have never seen or heard of leaders taking similar actions. And, I have never seen or heard of any organization bouncing back from change as quickly as did these hospitals.

Within days, the employees moved through their fear, anger, and grief and were holding productive conversations about a hoped-for future.

People feel grief when they experience loss; they feel nearly paralyzed when they feel they have lost control and have no idea what will happen next. They are angry when they feel betrayed. Their brains run rampant with worst-case scenarios and they have a difficult time mustering energy to do their daily tasks.

To counteract the effects of fear, anger, or resignation, people need to feel safe enough to fully express themselves without being judged. This doesn't fuel negativity; it creates the opportunity to find hope together.

One participant described the process of encouraging people to talk about how they feel as, "giving people the permission, language, and structure for bringing their entire self to work."

The younger generation in the workplace expects to express themselves fully. If they don't feel safe and respected, they'll go find a job down the street where they are treated like partners and enjoying their workday is a corporate value.

No longer can people be told to leave their emotions at the door. To stay competitive in today's world, organizations need to write steps for *building strong relationships that inspire employees* into their strategic plans. Procedures for hiring and promoting are also overdue for a change. A leader's interpersonal skills should rank higher than technical capability. Organizational cultures must be built on a foundation of trust and safety where leaders encourage discussions that explore how people feel about their work.

Daniel Kahneman, the 2002 winner of the Nobel Prize for Economics, said, "Business is more about emotions than most businesspeople care to admit. It's time to put the passion for work and the joy of creation back into business." People need to feel good about their work and the leaders they work for.

Are You Ready?

If you are uncomfortable with the idea of discussing emotions at work, know **the practice of outsmarting your brain does not mean you must learn how to *express* your emotions.** Using emotional intelligence in your conversations doesn't mean you are required to show any emotion beyond your comfort level. It also doesn't mean you are giving license to people to rage or complain at will.

> Learning how to be emotionally intelligent
> is the process of understanding how the
> brain works, and then using this information
> to choose how you want to think and act.

To make better decisions, stimulate your creativity, increase your persuasive powers, and live healthier, more peaceful lives, you must learn how to partner with the feelings that arise, not suppress them like you've been taught to do. When you become aware of what is going on in your brain and body and the reasons for your reactions, you will be better able to choose your emotional states. Then, the ability to receive, understand, and allow what others are experiencing will increase your relationship and leadership success.

This book will teach you how to apply reflective intelligence and emotional choice for personal development and improved interactions. Chapters 1 and 2 present scientific findings in a clear and usable format to help you detach from the power of your overly protective brain. Once you know how to take back control of your brain, the next chapters provide instructions and applications sprinkled with examples and stories to help you retrain your brain in a variety of circumstances.

If you practice the exercises in this book, you will learn how to stop your brain from driving you crazy. Hopefully, you will be inspired to make these practices part of your daily life. Outsmarting your brain is no easy task, but even small shifts will give you big results.

CHAPTER 1
WHO'S IN CHARGE?

Reason vs. Rationalization

Karl, my life partner, and I were rushing to catch a plane in Denver. We stopped to fill the tank of our rental car. When I tried to prepay with my credit card, nothing happened. I inserted the card a few more times, not so gently by the third try.

Karl came to see what was wrong. He began instructing me on the best way to insert the credit card, "If you try it a bit more slowly…"

I snapped, "I know how to do this," and gave him a look of disgust before stomping off to find the cashier. I discovered the computer had gone down. We had little time to get to another gas station before having to pay triple for the gas to the car rental company. I ran to the car and started the engine. Thankfully, Karl got the point and jumped in beside me.

Once we were on the move, I said to Karl, "I'm sorry for my reaction, for biting your head off when you tried to help me.

You see, I have this thing… when someone tells me how to do a simple task, especially one most people know how to do, I get angry. I'm working on not being so reactive, but I'm not sure I'm going to stop in this lifetime."

He said, "I understand," then smiled and continued, "and you know, I have this thing… I get anxious and want to help when I see someone is struggling, especially with a simple task. I'll work on my reactions, but I'm not sure I'm going to stop in this lifetime."

We both laughed. The tension melted away. I remembered why I felt Karl was the perfect partner for me.

We could have easily simmered in resentment for a while. I could have faulted him for being a clueless man. He could have stubbornly clung to being right for jumping in.

Our *excuses disguised as reasons* would have been logical or not-so logical rationalizations for behavior that would increase the tension. The more we stuck to our rationalizations, the more we would split apart. By stepping back and sharing what we thought triggered our reactions, we took responsibility for our words and behavior, admitting we have silly habits. The sharing and the laughter brought us back together.

After making an important decision, I often ask myself, "Do you have *a good reason or just a convenient rationalization* for what you are about to do?" This helps me step back and reflect before taking my next step. Asking myself this question is harder to do when intense emotions are triggered, but the more times I remember to ask, the more the question comes to me by habit.

I might not stop my emotions from being triggered in this lifetime, but I can work on stepping back and reflecting on what

I said and did once I sense an emotional shift. It helps me take back control from my reactive brain, improving my relationships and peace of mind.

Self-awareness leads to asking yourself the right questions. Self-awareness also increases empathy. You will see others and situations in a new light, providing fresh ideas on how to approach problems and conflicts.

Changing Your Mind Doesn't Make You Weak

Being emotionally triggered by events is a normal reaction. Your brain has been shaped by your life experiences. You don't have time to question everything you do, and the constant act of examining your thoughts would leave you feeling awkwardly self-conscious.

Neuroscientist Michael Gazzaniga says humans get stuck in automatic thought-processing and fool themselves into thinking they are acting consciously and willfully.[1] When someone asks you why you did something, you immediately come up with an ad hoc answer that fits the situation even if the response doesn't make complete sense. These instant and unconscious interpretations act to constrain the brain, limiting creativity, awareness of impact, and the freedom to choose to act differently.

In addition to instantly having a reason for your own reactions, you quickly assume you understand what people mean, want, and need without fact-checking your assumptions. You often form your opinions before they finish their thoughts, and then you react negatively when they don't agree with you.

Although the process is a difficult one to master, you can slow down and contemplate your reactions and viewpoints. You might not be able to tell your brain what to do, but you can thoughtfully consider what you will do next. You can change your mind.

The first step is willingness. You must accept you can change, and then commit to stopping and questioning your thoughts using a schedule until your brain creates a habit of self-awareness. You may be annoyed by this exercise. As Daniel Kahneman points out in his book, *Thinking Fast and Slow,* our brains don't like to work that hard.[2] We would rather believe our excuses instead.

While teaching a class on how to turn difficult conversations into positive results, a woman said, "People always want me to change the way I present my ideas. I am who I am. That's not going to change."

I sensed how protective she was of her style. I respectfully asked her to describe the results she now gets when she shares her ideas. She said, "I'm not winning most of my arguments. That is why they want me to change. I do good work on paper. I just can't get people to see what's best for them."

I asked her how she defined herself. She declared she was *the one who gets things done.* I asked her what she wanted from others. She said she wanted people to see the value in her ideas but when she got excited, they quit listening to her. She assumed they just didn't care as much as she did. I asked her if she would be willing to explore different ways of getting people to listen to her and buy into her ideas. She reluctantly agreed. I asked her if any of her peers cared *almost as much* as she did. She named two. I asked if people listened to these two people. She said "yes." We looked at the methods they used. She then willingly explored ways she could try some new approaches in a way that felt authentic to her own style. In the end, she agreed that other people did care, and that she could still get things done and be valued for her contribution with a few alterations in her style.

The exercise worked because she was willing to step back and explore her assumptions, especially what she thought she couldn't change. On her own, she had been defending herself for years. She angrily reacted to feedback, as many people do. We started the practice of outsmarting her brain in the class. Hopefully, she would continue the practice of opening her mind after the class ended.

Admitting to what isn't working well for you, and then deciding to drop old ideas, take on a different perspective, and act differently is difficult to do on your own. You can get better at reflection and self-awareness with practice. This book will show you how. Remember, you aren't giving in. You are exercising free will.

Physicist David Bohm said the tendency to cling to how we see the world and our opinions is a hedge against our fear of not knowing.[3] Your brain wants you to feel safe and comfortable in a known world. Connecting with others happens when you have the courage to let go of assumptions so new perspectives and ideas can emerge. The three words, "I don't know" are very powerful. They allow you to then say, "Let me think about this." When you open yourself to examining and changing your thoughts, reactions, and behaviors, you are more open to listening, connecting, and creating with others.

To do this, you need to understand what you need and what the people you are with need, too. You then want to notice your typical reactions when your needs are not met, or you fear they won't be met. These are the crucial steps to take to outsmart your brain.

Common Sense, But Not Common Practice

If mastering emotional reactions and learning how to factor the needs of others into conversations are so important, why are emotions not talked about in the workplace? Most cultures champion technical prowess in schools, and organizations prioritize technical achievement when hiring and promoting. Emotions do not show up in the language of report cards and performance reviews except when they are hidden in comments such as "she has a poor attitude" and "he has difficulty taking feedback from anyone."

Thus, we are inadequately trained in getting along with others at work and at home. The focus on the technical and intellectual aspects of work hinders success by limiting collaboration and creativity.

The real travesty is that you naturally have immediate access to your emotional needs. When you were young, you knew what you felt and what you wanted. Babies quickly respond to what makes them happy and sad. Toddlers are particularly sensitive to the feelings of others.

As you grew up, you were taught to deny this intelligence. You were cautioned by your parents and teachers to be practical. You learn from your peers that when you show love and compassion, you could end up feeling rejected, humiliated, and sad. You should never cry. You should hide your fears. This conditioning makes you distrust the messages you get from the emotional centers of our brain. At some point, you may have learned how to ignore these messages altogether.

Now, as adults, when you go to work:

1. You don't heed what our "gut" tells you to do.
2. You are careful not to let your heart rule your mind.
3. You strive to keep a "stiff upper lip" because displays of emotions make you look weak.

These habits block your ability to use emotional information when you make decisions and communicate with others. Ask most people how they feel and they say, "Fine." Some respond with no emotion. Others reveal their true state in the inflection and volume of their voice. Few people stop to assess their condition. Of those who do, most think twice before telling the truth about how they feel unless they are feeling great. Though many people yearn to express how upset they are—how angry or afraid they feel—they remain tight-lipped, secretly hoping the asker will sense their pain and inquire with compassion about what they need.

In short, you weren't taught in school how to use the wisdom of your emotions. Then you grow up and experience a high level of anxiety at work. You might be able to attend standard courses in conflict resolution and handling stress. You might even attend an anger management course. These classes are generally limited to one-day "fix-it" programs, quickly forgotten when under pressure back on the job. And, if you are a manager, you probably don't even show up for class unless someone higher than you mandated you attend.

I rarely find a company interested in the investment needed to train its employees or leaders to recognize and constructively talk about how they feel and use their emotions on the job. Even fewer want to teach how to encourage emotional expression in others so people can better understand and work together.

Most people don't even have the literacy to define how they feel when asked. There might be an academic discourse around emotions when prompted to look at past interactions, but most people struggle when asked to name what they are experiencing in the present moment.

> Our cognitive brains have lost touch with
> the emotion expressed in our bodies except
> in extreme cases of excitement or pain.
> We miss important data and, even worse, have
> learned to numb ourselves to our senses.

Prior to attending classes I teach that include emotional awareness, I have participants complete the inventory in Appendix A called *"Name that Emotion."* The instructions ask you to stop at four intervals throughout the day and write:

1. what you are feeling, and
2. what do you think is the source of your feeling?

You have a list of nearly eighty emotions to help you articulate what you are feeling.

Most people struggle with the exercise at first. They dislike taking the time out from their work and can't differentiate one type of happiness, fear, or anger from another.

After a few days, the exercise gets easier. Those who continually mark their charts notice distinctions and begin to identify patterns in their reactions. They write words such as confused, delighted, embarrassed, or depleted without looking at the list. They feel more in control of their emotions simply by taking the time to check in with themselves.

Awareness is the first step. Once you can label the emotions you feel, you can more easily shift your emotional state if you choose to. Chapter 3 offers techniques for shifting instead of stuffing your emotions away. Or, you can accept the emotion you are feeling as a relevant expression in your current situation. The power lies in making the conscious choice of how you want to feel, which is fully within your power to do.

EXERCISE #1—Name that emotion

Start a daily practice of using the inventory *in* Appendix A, *Name that Emotion*. Notice what you are feeling and write the words in the charts. Fill out the chart four times a day for two weeks. As you familiarize yourself with your emotional states, you will better understand their effect on your behavior, including your productivity, confidence, and happiness. Then, when you learn more about what triggers your reactions and what other choices you can make in the next chapter, you will be freer to choose how you want to feel and act in all circumstances.

> Between stimulus and response,
> there is a space.
> In that space is our power to
> choose our response.
> In our response lies our growth
> and our freedom.
> —Viktor Frankl, *Man's Search for Meaning*

CHAPTER 2
DEVELOPING AWARENESS

Head Games

A few years ago, I taught a series of seminars at a chemical company. Between classes, I provided coaching for the managers to implement what they learned in class. After the first session, Larry, one of the managers, forwarded me an email he had received from a peer. The email was a copy of a message Larry sent to his colleague, Sarah. She replied by copying his original message and typing in her comments in red capital letters next to his statements. Most of her comments started with the word, "WRONG."

Larry wanted me to agree that Sarah was rude and out to get him. He was crafting a scathing email to send back to Sarah proving she was wrong and ill-informed. Fortunately, he called me before hitting the send button.

I asked him, "Are you absolutely sure her only purpose in writing the email was to prove you are an idiot?"

He reluctantly answered that there could be a possibility of something else on her mind.

I said, "What else is going on that could possibly shed some light on her behavior?"

He said he wasn't sure.

"Be creative," I suggested. "What do you think prompted Sarah to do this? What else could be making her upset with you or this situation?"

Larry said, "Obviously, she is mad, either at me or at someone else. I guess we should talk about that, not about who is screwing up the report."

I was then able to coach Larry on how he could best approach this conversation with his colleague, starting with asking her if she was willing to find another way to handle disagreements with him other than through email which can be easily misunderstood.

Larry contacted me a day later to tell me what happened. He said he told her how he was feeling about her remarks. After a long, awkward pause, Sarah told him she thought she was responsible for choosing the deadline dates, not him. She felt Larry didn't trust her to do it and was trying to undermine her authority. After convincing her that he wanted to work with her and not against her, they realized they needed to define who was responsible for what parts of the project. They agreed on some areas and negotiated others. They were now respectfully working together.

From our coaching, I knew that the next time Larry received an email with emotional overtones, he would be more inclined to look for the meaning beneath the words before reacting negatively to the anger he felt.

Larry was upset by the way Sarah's comments were made. By taking the time to look below the surface for meaning, he found his colleague had her own emotions triggered by his original email. She had to protect the position she thought was being undermined. She wasn't thinking how her actions would make Larry feel, making the problem worse.

A clash of reactions can poison a working relationship. By calling me, Larry opened himself to change his pattern of reacting. He was then able to find out what was really upsetting his colleague. This allowed him to have a conversation that cleared the way to seeing solutions.

What does it take to change your reactive patterns?

The first step is to clear your mental clutter out of the way. You must stop the noise in your brain before you can identify your feelings and assumptions. Once you see the source of your own reactions, you can then determine what you want to feel, say, and do next.

Before we go on, let me explain that what you are about to read runs counter to some therapies and self-help books where behavioral change is based on changing thought patterns: *Change your thoughts, you change your behavior.* This technique may work well in some situations. For most situations where strong emotions are involved, you will fail at *rescripting* the dialogue that runs in your head. Even if you can force yourself to talk or act differently, the change doesn't last. Then you mentally beat yourself up for failing to control yourself, which hinders your growth and success.

Before you try to change your thoughts, you first need to identify the physical reactions in the body that created the feelings and thoughts. That is why you started with Exercise #1 where you began noticing and naming the emotions you feel. The next step is to determine what was said or done that "triggered" the biochemical and hormonal reaction that shows up as an emotional state. It takes an awareness of your emotional triggers to override their power.

Neuroscientist Antonio Damasio, author of *Looking for Spinoza: Joy, Sorrow, and the Feeling Brain,* says that at any moment, your rate of breathing, blood flow, tension in your muscles, and constriction in your gut represents a pattern in your brain that you identify as a feeling.[1] When you understand the source of your physical reactions, you have the information to make decisions and resolve your interpersonal misunderstandings.

You may even look at your feelings and thoughts as symptoms that lead you to the emotional source. When you identify the source, you can consciously choose how you want to behave next instead of defending your unconscious reactions. By paying attention to your feelings, you can become the master not the victim of your reactions.

Additionally, when you understand that your emotions are preconscious biological reflexes that trigger thoughts and reactions, and that your brain then will direct you to act in ways it perceives to be constructive in the heat of the moment, it becomes easier to say, "I'm sorry" and make amends. Breaking habits is still difficult, but you will find letting go and trying out new behaviors to be easier than in the past. You may even forgive yourself for being human.

The Three Brains

Outsmarting your brain starts with looking at how the brain functions. If you track how sensory input travels through the brain, you will find an intricate system that first operates at a precognition level, meaning there is much going on outside of your awareness. In fact, the logical brain is the last to be activated when input from external sources is processed.

This isn't an accident of nature. The brain's motto is "Survival First!" The design came into existence when "eat or be eaten" and propagation of the species were truly the priorities of the day. The brain's primary function is to keep the body, and the species, alive.

Over time, the brain developed to help you deal with modern life. This did not change the priority "protect and propagate" even though these words take on a different meaning in today's world. The patterns hardwired into your neural circuitry are still following the rules of threat and reward. Fortunately, you also have a moral framework that helps you make decisions that support living in communities. You have three major centers in your brain—with two operating at the precognitive level—that constantly interact as you go about your day.

The Reactive Brain

The base, or the first brain, is called the **reactive or reptilian brain.** More commonly known as the brain stem, this portion of the brain resembles the brain found in reptiles.

The reptilian brain is the command center for living, regulating your sleep and waking, respiration, body temperature, and reactive movements needed to keep you alive. Consider how

THE THREE BRAINS

3. Cognitive/Thinking
Brain
Short-term memory
Feeling identification
Reflection/Analysis
CHOICE

2. Mammalian/
Social Brain
Long-term memory
Emotions
EGO/Identity

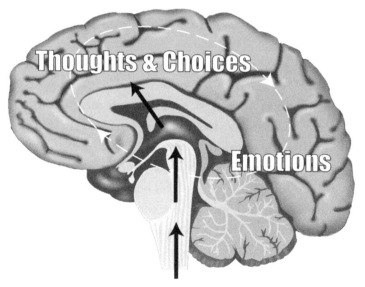

Thoughts & Choices

Emotions

Perception Triggers Reaction

1. Reptilian/Reactive Brain
Protection/Desire
Maintenance of body
Survival of species

difficult it is to concentrate on a task when you are too cold or hungry to do anything. Your brain wants you to take care of your physical needs so you can survive long enough to carry out your brilliant plans.

Next, the reactive brain is on the lookout for what could physically harm you. It operates in a state of hyperalert, a loyal sentinel constantly surveying the environment. If safe, the brain then hunts for what might give you physical pleasure. The reactive brain is constantly asking these three questions:

1. Can it hurt me? If the answer is no...
2. Can I eat it? If the answer is no...
3. Can I have sex with it?

Note: It's possible that the order of the questions is different for some people as my students often point out to me. I haven't found enough evidence to either argue against or agree with them. However, I can't help but smile at their wisdom.

Responses to the three questions are automatic before you have a chance to think. Your heart beats fast, you get goose bumps, your hair stands on end, you smile, snarl, avert your eyes, laugh, or slump without thinking. Consider how you jump when someone unexpectedly enters a room, how you gravitate toward the appetizing smell of food cooking, how you straighten up when you see your boss, how you shudder at the sight of a police car, and how you tingle inside when someone attractive stands close to you and smiles. Based on your upbringing and experiences, you judge the sensations happening in your body as good or bad and react accordingly. Your training and experiences, which include learning life lessons, continue to alter your programming, affecting the intensity of the biochemical reactions and subsequent behavior. You create a personalized dread and reward system that mutates over time.

This is the reason why you trust nonverbal messages over the spoken word. Facial expressions, gestures, postures, and symbols trigger the threat and reward reactor. You may be good at suppressing emotions, but you can't stop the instant reactions generated from your reactive brain.

When, and if, the reactive brain is triggered, you will flight, fight, or seek to feast or fornicate. You may be more civilized than reptiles, based on the rules and laws you learned growing up, but your body still reacts to stimuli through this brain first. Much of your behavior is based either on the fear of being hurt or on the desire to make yourself feel good.

The more active you are, the more vigilant is your brain. This includes checking your cell phone, getting news updates, and dealing with uncontrollable traffic, noise, weather, and bad air. Depending on circumstances, you might experience a constant level of stress nearly every day.

Adding to environmental stressors, when someone looks like they are about to say something that will hurt your feelings, test your authority, or make you feel stupid, your brain reacts the same way as if you received a physical threat. The brain prepares you to flight or fight, signaling the body to release adrenalin, increase the blood flow in your large muscle groups, and direct your attention to seek a means of protection.

Your thoughts are distorted by this defense mechanism. Your brain looks for ways to rid itself of the stress caused by the reaction. You say things you wish you hadn't or forget what you rehearsed so diligently to say. Your physical reactions fall in the range anywhere from violence to quickly leaving the scene. Without recognizing what is happening in your body, and then consciously relaxing your body and shifting your emotional state, it is nearly impossible to objectively assess what is going on.

In fact, the brain is constantly fabricating a portion of what you think is reality. In protection mode, you predict what is going to happen and begin to react before people enter the room. You are prone to illusion based on speculation. You then swear you saw something occur that didn't happen or heard someone say something they didn't because you distort what you perceive based on your predictions.

While your brain is busy fabricating details, it is also busy filtering out what you perceive as noise. You miss input that your brain determines isn't important. You quickly forget what you unconsciously deem irrelevant.

It is no wonder two people can argue endlessly about what they each swear happened in the past. They perceived very different events even though they stood in the same place.

Additionally, when your brain senses a major threat, parts of your brain shut down, hindering your ability to store new information. You may focus and act fast when driven by fear or anger. Yet you struggle with change and learning new ways to behave when stressed. Your brain reacts without thinking, fearfully or aggressively, to keep things status quo.

All of this adds up to humans being stimulated more than any other animal. The body can't assimilate the overload of chemicals secreted when operating in prolonged protection mode. The result is what we've come to know as "burnout."

Adrenalin and cortisol triggered by stress wear out the body, causing high blood pressure, heart disease, ulcers, hormonal imbalances, a host of digestive problems, and a weakened immune system.

> The first step in outsmarting your
> brain is being aware of what triggers
> your protective reactions.

You must learn how to focus on the present moment to sense when your brain perceives danger. You must partner with your feelings instead of trying to hide them. Recognizing your feelings comes first; then you can determine what caused the emotional reaction in the body, whether the source is external (what you perceive and sense) or internal (what you are thinking about that is causing you to feel a certain way).

If you choose not to feel—to deny the existence of an emotional state—you are ignoring, not ending, the reaction. You merely disconnect your brain from your body. Your body still suffers. To bring more peace, creativity, and health into your life, you must heed your feelings so you can begin to discern what is a real threat from what is not. Your practice will shift the wiring in this portion of your brain so you react less often or with less intensity. The tips at the end of this chapter will help.

The Social Brain

Once input is processed by the reptilian brain, it enters the **mammalian or limbic system, also known as the social brain** because it evolved to help you deal with the social world of humans. However, the development of this portion of the brain can still be traced to the purpose of survival.

Humans, like other mammals, need to nurture their young. Reptilian babies are born fully functional with the ability to run from their parents who are likely to eat them. Our babies can't run; they can't survive at all without help. Survival of our species requires adults care for babies. Thus, you have the capacity to care, which includes caring enough to feed your babies even when you are tired, to protect them even when you are afraid, and to want them to learn to be on their own even when you feel the loss of them moving on.

You also need to count on others to survive, so you have hormonal and biochemical reactions that encourage you to have at least one friend, if not a full community. Studies show longevity and health can be linked to the number and depth of friendships a person has. Isolation is the worst form of punishment. Loneliness registers in the body as real pain.

With the needs to care for and protect came a cascade of emotional states including what is labeled as jealousy, delight, remorse, gratitude, grief, anger, and love. We cry, we kiss, we groom each other, we bicker, we steal, we defend, we cuddle, we console, we beam with pride, and we cower in embarrassment based on our needs to socially connect, care about others, and be cared for.

All humans in every culture laugh, cry, and express emotions through facial expressions and posture. You instinctively know what emotional expressions are trustworthy regardless of the spoken word. Emotions are the foundation of our survival.

Your emotions are triggered by your social needs. As psychologist Abraham Maslow taught us in his classic and still relevant 1943 paper, *A Theory of Human Motivation,* there is a hierarchy of needs that drives your behavior.[2] You need air, food, water, shelter, and safety from physical harm to exist. Then you need love and a sense of belonging, followed by being accepted and valued by others, before you can feel fulfilled at the higher intellectual levels. You feel happy and content when your basic needs are met. You emotionally react if they are not.

There is another important structure housed in the social brain that helps you function daily—ego. To define who you are and make sense of the world around you, your brain develops constructs and rules that you protect without much thought. This is your ego—your sense of self and the map of the world you call reality.

All your life experiences and cumulative knowledge have created the frames that define your ego, especially what you have discovered that has helped you succeed, or at least what you think will get you through a day with as little trouble as possible. You seek activities that support your self-image. If you're told to think or act in a way that counters what your brain has determined is best for you and how you define your world, you resist, defending your sense of self and the world you think you live in.

So, the social brain is the next filter in line after the reactive brain. If what you perceive externally passes through the "foe, food, or fondle" test, it then travels through the minefield of emotional triggers related to your social connections and identity before it can be processed logically.

When your emotions are triggered, a host of neural, bio-chemical, and hormonal actions are initiated based on what your brain perceives you need to feel happy or satisfied. These needs can be defined by what you expect and desire. Based on what has helped you survive and succeed up to this point in your life, **you expect, believe you deserve, or desire to receive some of the following items, and react when your needs aren't met.**

Needs/Emotional Triggers

acceptance	respect
to be liked	to feel needed
to be understood	to feel valued
to be in control	to be right
to be included	freedom
comfort	attention
peacefulness	balance
consistency	order
new challenges	love
safety	predictability
fairness	fun
autonomy	to win
achievement	to make a difference
independence	accuracy

Some of these needs are important to you, others hold no emotional charge. You might discover other needs not identified here that bother you if the need isn't met; the list is not conclusive. You will also find other people have triggers different from yours. Your greatest strengths are what you end up protecting through flight- or fight-based reactions.

EXERCISE #2—Claim your triggers

Identify your top three to five triggers, meaning that you feel angry, upset, irritated, defensive, resentful, disappointed, hardened, sad, shut down, hurt, or a related feeling when:

1. it's likely you won't get this need met;
2. the person, group, or situation didn't give this to you but should have; or
3. it appears you have an opportunity to prove you deserve this need or this is your chance to fight for getting this need met.

NOTE: *Needs are not bad.* The reason you have these needs is because, at some point in your life, the need served you. Your needs are based on what has helped you be successful in life so far. For example, you may have found that **taking control** of situations and leading the way to find solutions has helped you advance in your career. You may regularly spend time learning because your wisdom has been critical to your work. It feels good **being right.** Maybe you enjoy the **appreciation** of your family so you do special things they enjoy. However, the more you become attached to these needs—to being the one in control, the one who is right, or being appreciated—the more you will react when your brain decides that someone is trying to take control from you, make you wrong, or doesn't appreciate your contribution. Then your needs become emotional triggers.

> Your greatest strengths are your most
> vulnerable triggers. What has helped
> you succeed in this life is what your
> brain most wants to protect.

Be honest with yourself. Which three to five needs, when not met, most likely trigger a reaction in you? Identify the needs that you hold most dear.

You might find it hard to choose just five items, but if you don't limit the number, it will be difficult to discern which need is triggering an emotional reaction. The goal is to notice when you are reacting so you can ask yourself what your brain thinks you didn't get that you should have.

If you practice Exercise #1 from the last chapter, you will teach yourself to notice when your heart beats faster, your breathing shortens, your muscles tighten, or you yearn to run out the door. The sooner you recognize the shift in your biological state, the quicker you can discern what need your brain thinks is missing when you practice Exercise #2.

Most behavior is driven by a desire to
avoid pain, sorrow, or shame, or on the
quest for pleasure, comfort, or pride. You
physically and mentally respond to the
possibility of loss or reward before you
can logically process what is going on.

When people act in ways that don't meet your expectations or desires, the biochemical trigger happens in a blink of an eye. Your brain jumps into defensive mode, acting to protect you from people who may not feel you are worthy of being listened to, people who may not like you, and people who may not think you are smart, talented, or in some way worthwhile. If you don't react in anger, you probably retreat, avoiding the risk. These reactions can ruin your day, and even your life, depending on what you choose to do *after* you react.

Once you notice you are reacting, even slightly, you can ask yourself, "Is the person or group intentionally denying or ignoring my need or am I taking the situation too personally?" If you are worrying or speculating about an event that hasn't occurred, ask, "How do I know I won't get what I need? Is it critical I get this need met? What will happen if I don't?" If it's true that someone is snubbing your need or blocking you from achieving it, can you either ask for what you need or, if it doesn't matter, can you let the need go?

For example, I was asked to create a report for the CEO but handed it to my boss first. My boss flipped through the report I painstakingly created. When he saw the budget, he pointed to one item and suggested I leave it out for now. I quickly defended the item. An argument ensued. Finally, I told him I would think about it, and said, "Maybe you're right, but you didn't give me any feedback on the report."

He said, "You always do a good job, do I have to tell you?"

This was my chance to ask for what I needed. "Yes," I replied, "I need to hear that now and then."

He reacted by saying, "You never tell me when I do a good job."

Of course, my boss had needs, too! I said he was right and I was sorry for the oversight. We awkwardly acknowledged each other for the next few weeks until the praise came more naturally for real reasons. Because I had the courage to ask for what I needed, I created the opportunity for my boss to ask for what he needed as well.

The steps for getting your needs met or for releasing needs if they aren't that important will be further described in Chapter 3 on *Activating Choice*.

Without acknowledging the need that is triggering the emotional reaction, you become enslaved to the need. On the other hand, if you honestly declare your needs—that you had expected people to treat you in a particular way and had anticipated events would unfold as you had hoped—you will begin to see life and your relationships more objectively. From this perspective, you are freer to choose what to do after you react.

Even internally generated percepts—what you are thinking about—loop through the limbic system. When you think about a need you didn't get or worry that you won't get what you need, you detonate your rage, push your panic button, or fall down a spiral of depression. If you catch yourself cooking mush in your brain, you can consciously shift your focus to generate feelings of gratitude, pride, determination, courage, and joy at will. The practice of being self-aware comes first. Then you can work on identifying how to get your needs met, or let them go for now, to fully outsmart your brain.

The Thinking Brain

The rise of civilization drove the need to discern the impact of one's behavior on others, to test perception against what else could be possible, and to shift thoughts to either a darker or brighter mode even in the face of adversity. Thus, the third brain, known as the **thinking or cortical brain,** evolved to give you the ability to discern right from wrong, good from bad, and determine how current behavior could affect the future. The thinking brain gives you the ability to sit back and analyze what you think is going on. It also gives you the unique capacity to make plans both rationally and imaginatively.

One of the important features of the thinking brain is short-term memory, the "container" in which you mix present input with long-term memory, which allows you to reason, learn, and create. Combined with your need to be social, the development of the thinking brain led to the existence of the arts, religion, and science. Riane Eisler said in her classic book about our cultural evolution, *The Chalice and the Blade,* of all the life forms, "...only we can plant and harvest fields, compose poetry and music, seek truth and justice, and teach a child to read."

Yet, our development would not have happened had it not been driven by emotions first; by the passion, envy, anger, terror, love, excitement, curiosity, compassion, competition, and even vengeance that inspired new ideas and actions. Thus, you can add many Fs to the fight, flight, feast, and fornicate formula. Now you have family and favoritism, fastidiousness and fickleness, falsity and feistiness, fulfilled and fortunate, fantasy and formula, and a sense of fun. Humans can joke, lie, create, and regret dreams all in one conversation.

However, as with many things in life, a great blessing is also a grave curse. You can seek truth, beauty, and justice while competing, waging war, and destroying what is valued by others. You can be compassionate and cruel, kind and ruthless, and affectionate and disloyal, depending on how you feel and what your brain deems is most important.

So, input is processed through the reactive and social brains before it gets to the thinking brain. The brain is always surveying the territory for dangers, being ever-alert to possible blows to your body and your ego.

In addition, your thoughts are also processed by looping through the emotional brain and back into the thinking brain. Thus, you can create an emotional loop where you work yourself into anger, fear, depression, and frustration without external stimuli. Your thoughts and memories can trigger emotional states just as effectively as someone else's words or actions.

The thinking brain thrives on making sense of what is going on as quickly as possible. It is a meaning-making machine. It must find a reason for your emotional reactions even if the reaction is not defensible. The thinking brain is also a master at guessing and exaggerating. Essentially, your thinking brain is very effective at making things up so you feel like you know exactly what you are doing.

> The rational, thinking brain is also the
> irrational, rationalizing, justifying brain.

The thinking brain is capable of activating emotional intelligence. With your growing awareness of what is going on in all three of your brains, you can outsmart your brain. You can sense your reactions, interrogate your thinking, assess if what you perceive poses a threat or reward, *really.* You can achieve success by comparing your mental chatter to the reality of the situation, discerning between what you have the power to change and what you do not, and then choose ways to cope and adjust. You can discover what motivates you to see new approaches and possibilities. You can become the master of your mental processes instead of being the slave.

When you outsmart your brain, you see options when you thought you had no choice. You hear the true voice of wisdom over the noise of self-talk without the silence of suppression. You feel the power of overseeing your brain instead of letting it overrun you. Life lightens up. The road is clear. It is easier to figure out what you need to do as you lay out all the choices you have.

■ *Practical Tips*

1. As you did in Chapter 1, keep tracking your emotional states using the form in Appendix A.

2. Use your trigger list to help you consider the source of your emotions. Remember, you may be feeling more than one emotion at any given time. It doesn't matter whether you feel good or bad, try to discover what your brain perceives you need in the situation. Notice when your needs are being met as well as when they are not acknowledged. Write your triggers on the chart.

3. Identify the three most common triggers of emotions that drain you. For the next three weeks, notice when these needs drive your emotions, thoughts, and behavior. When you see some patterns, ask yourself what you can do to get your needs met or what you need to do to let go of a need if getting it met is not possible under the present circumstances of your work or life. Then create a plan for how you will get your needs met in the future.

> Anyone can become angry—that is easy.
> But to be angry with the right person,
> to the right degree, at the right time,
> for the right purpose in the right way—
> that is not easy."
> —*Aristotle, the Nicomachean Ethics*

CHAPTER 3
ACTIVATING YOUR POWER OF CHOICE

The Art of Suppression

The thinking brain gives you the ability to suppress your emotions and rationalize your reactions so you can swiftly justify your nonproductive behavior. Feelings—how you label the emotional reactions in your body—are often stuffed away in a blink of an eye. You can become so adept at suppression that you cut off your ability to express your feelings. You also limit your capacity to be aware of, understand, and appreciate the feelings of others.

Children are schooled early in the art of suppression. They are taught that uncomfortable emotions such as fear, anger, and frustration are unacceptable to express. The neural pathways from the cognitive to the emotional brain atrophy, weakening the ability to experience all emotions, including joy and love. The late Israeli Prime Minister Golda Meir said, "Those who don't know how to weep with their whole hearts don't know how to laugh, either." Have you ever wondered what happened to the excitement you felt when you started your career? You biologically "numbed-out."

Also, the more you suppress feelings in your younger years, the less you socially interact with ease as you age. The source of many failed marriages is one or both partners' inability to identify their feelings.

> The more you practice self-control and the suppression of painful emotions, the more you lose touch with positive emotions, including happiness and passion. Life becomes gray as you age.

However, you didn't become an unemotional robot. There are still emotional reactions being triggered in your body. You have become good at willing yourself to ignore the flow of energy inside you, giving no voice to your feelings. If a strong emotion pops up, you hold it in until you can't take it any longer, raging in traffic, insulting the people you care the most about, and looking for ways to make your colleagues wrong or less in value than you whenever you can. If you achieved mastery in quarantining your reactions, you take them out on yourself. Your anger or stress simmers just below the surface, wreaking havoc on your health and confidence.

You can reteach your brain to feel. Since the wiring in your brain is malleable and new connections are made each day based on what you learn and experience, it is not too late to reverse the suppression process. You can increase your awareness of your emotional patterns and triggers and your sensitivity to what others are feeling by practicing the exercises in this book.

Does this mean you must run around expressing your feelings? A leader in one of my classes told me he was afraid of turning his meetings into sensitivity groups. I told him the point is not to share what you feel for the sake of expression, but to give meaning to your actions and to make it safe for others to express their ideas and feelings. If you aren't comfortable with your own emotions, you will send signals to others that they aren't safe expressing themselves with you. This will stop them from saying anything that could trigger your displeasure, protecting themselves from feeling wrong, embarrassed, or hurt.

When you accept your own reactions, and then shift to feeling more curious, accepting, and calm, you increase the psychological safety in the room. When with you, people will be more open to learning, will think more creatively, and be more willing to resolve conflicts.

> Instead of managing your emotions, when you notice how you feel, you will be better able to understand your triggers and then shift your emotions if you choose to.

One of the exercises I use when I teach emotional intelligence is to pair people up and have one person recount the events of the day before. The listener has been given a page full of emotions. They are instructed to, every ten seconds, give a different emotion for the storyteller to express while talking about the day before, even if he or she must alter the story to fit the feeling. The trick is for the storyteller to access the feelings without thinking, to act them out before judgment creeps in. With a little warming up, everyone jumps into the game. By the end of the exercise, the room is full of laughter.

The point of the exercise is for people to know they can access any emotions if they choose to. They can shift to feeling something different at will.

In one of my classes, a production manager, Allen, spoke in a monotone while attempting to do the exercise. No matter how much I coaxed him, he refused to alter his expression. When he finished, he told me he was a calm guy by nature. Nothing bothered him. He said he was not attending my class for himself, but to find ways to help those who worked for him to better deal with their emotions.

I commended him for his mastery, but then I asked if any person or situation ever pushed his buttons. He said nothing, not even an aggressive employee, bothered him. "I just handle it," he said. "Getting upset isn't worth my time. I am better at solving problems when I stay neutral."

Again, I applauded his skill. I agreed that a neutral tone improved conflict resolution. I asked him if he had a mentor or a good book that acted as his guide. I had never met anyone who had truly reached this level of consciousness without years of guidance and practice, and probably a lot of meditation.

He shook his head in denial.

"Let me ask you two more questions," I said. "If you still feel the same way about your temperament, then I'll admit to being wrong."

Allen agreed.

"When you told your story, you mentioned taking your son to play soccer. I gathered he is a decent player. Can you tell me about the last time he played so well, you burst out screaming and clapping for him?"

Allen sat quietly for a moment before he said, "It's been a few years."

"And, when was the last time you rolled around on the floor with him, laughing so hard it hurt?" I asked.

This time his silence seemed like it went on forever. Finally, he said, "Okay, I got it."

After class, Allen asked me coach him for a few months. In between sessions, he practiced listening to his body to notice any shifts that could represent an emotion. During our sessions, he shared what he was learning about himself. We repeated the storytelling exercise at the end of the third month of coaching, giving himself a chance to express himself more fully.

By the end of our coaching, Allen could tell his soccer story as if he were a Shakespearean actor. He reported not only a richness of experience in his home life, but a new depth of possibilities in his work assignments and relationships. It doesn't take much to open your mind and heart.

Don't try to manage your emotions.
Instead, acknowledge their presence.
You can always choose to feel something else
if you think it will help you in the moment.

Don't be afraid to be fully alive and present. Notice your emotions, their source, and their significance. Then you can choose the best course of action in the moment, whether you want to make a direct request or to find a way to release (not suppress) the emotions and go on.

Making Your Own Movie

In *Handle with Care: The Emotional Intelligence Activity Book*,[1] the definition of awareness is "...the capacity to stand apart from ourselves and examine our thinking, our intentions, our behaviors, and our effects on what is around us." If you could, at any moment, stop and watch yourself as if you were in a movie, hearing both your verbal and mental dialogue as you observe your actions, what would you notice? You might witness a wonderful comedy. Emotional intelligence can be measured by how quickly you can laugh at yourself.

Since the Greek root of the word "intelligence" means "to make a choice among options," you access your emotional intelligence when you recognize there are different emotions you can choose to feel. You are in control even if you choose to be angry, sad, or afraid. When you identify a feeling and what triggered it, you are then free to 1) choose how you want to feel and 2) consider possible actions to take based on the outcome that would best serve your needs and desires as well as what others might need from you.

It is good practice to first choose how you want to feel before you choose what you might say or do next to get your needs met.

If you choose to feel more calm and confident, you will make your decisions about what to do and say with a clearer mind.

You may choose to stay with the emotions you recognize. Sometimes you need to let people know you are disappointed with them. You might use your anger to launch a big change in your life. Many great things have happened based on the power of, 'Oh yeah, I'll show you." You might choose to stay sad so you can fully grieve the loss of a friend, a dream, or a physical ability.

Emotions aren't bad; they are reactions to stimuli. They reflect energy moving through the body. Acknowledging your emotions will help you discover what you need to break through blocks, make good decisions, and take a positive step forward. When you learn to listen to and accept your emotional states, you are better equipped to appreciate the expression of emotions in others, allowing them to safely express themselves when working things out with you.

Be careful to notice when you are deliberately choosing to stay with a feeling instead of justifying your reaction. Catch yourself saying, "I deserve to be mad because…" or "I am who I am, I don't need to change for anyone." The more you are attached to your story and your *rightful* reaction, the harder it is to shift your emotion.

The greater the intensity of the emotion and your justification for your reaction, the more difficult it is to shift how you feel. Difficult, but not impossible. Will your current emotional state help you achieve your desired outcome? If not, consider shifting to feeling something else. If you choose to shift, you can.

Ask yourself, "How do I want this story to end?"
Choose to feel the emotion that will
help you stand the higher ground and
achieve your desired outcome.

Recall the last argument you had. Did your emotions keep you stuck, unable to find common ground to work from? Could opening your mind or heart have helped you listen? Remember the time at work when you were worried, disappointed, or resentful about decisions made that affected you but you had no input? How easy was it for you to move forward, hoping for the best? Could a shift in emotions have helped you get through that troubled time?

Think about *who you are being* in your relationships at home and at work. Is the role you are playing affecting how you feel and act? Are you stuck or can you change your habits of interaction? Can you choose to feel compassion over judgment? Can you shift to feeling curious when you are annoyed? Can you summon hope to override your fear? Is there music or a memory that can calm you when you feel impatient? Can you call forth courage to battle your reluctance? You aren't giving in when you shift, you are gaining both better results and peace of mind.

The Optimal Productive State

If you want to be more creative, productive, and successful, your goal should be to feel more happiness, pride, and hope. I'm not suggesting you suppress other emotions, but shifting your emotions will help you achieve your goals. A good daily dose of laughter will also help.

Emotions affect your reasoning; you perceive things differently under the influence of your emotions. When you shift to feeling happier, you turn up your mental thermostat, producing the biochemicals that increase ease, efficiency, and rapidity of the operations in the neural network. You think more clearly and make quicker connections, leading to new ideas and solutions. Positive emotions stimulate the creative process. Gratitude, appreciation, hope, compassion, and love bring the major systems of the body into harmony. The rhythm of the brain synchronizes with the heart. Opening your heart heightens your intuitive clarity along with a greater sense of well-being.

When the body experiences a pleasurable reaction, the blood freely circulates through the brain, feeding creativity and the ability to focus on the task at hand. If the brain isn't fixated on protecting you, your ego, and your needs, you can use your mental resources to interact with the present moment. You see more details and options. You get more things done. You learn best when you are laughing and enjoying yourself. You are most alive when you are feeling good.

> You are at your best when your
> spirit feels nourished.

In contrast, the more obsessive emotions like anger, frustration, fear, stress, and resentment yield negative results.[2] Stress hormones divert blood from the brain to your large muscle groups to prepare you for action. Your heart speeds up, your breathing becomes shallow, your muscles tense up, your digestion is disrupted, and your thoughts turn toward protection and limiting loss. Feelings such as disappointment, boredom, and resignation slow your metabolism. You don't feel like working. You might not want to get out of bed. Even if you want to get work done, your brain is trying to rebalance your internal systems, borrowing from the available energy you would otherwise use to be productive.

If you allow stressful emotions to persist over time, you might decrease your capacity to think. You see fewer options, your memory declines, and you make more mistakes. You get sick more often, impacting your output. Your temperament declines. To cope, you might go numb, feeling as few emotions as you can.

In general, anger, overwhelm, and frustration handicap your brain. Fear washes out the creative center. Try to appreciate the challenge you are faced with to fully engage your brain under adverse conditions.

Stress can focus your attention and move you into action, but only in small doses. Your brain can only maintain an adrenalin-fed intensity for short periods of time. Stimulants like caffeine can amp you up, but eventually the body needs a rest. Your brain and your compromised immune system will force you to take a recess if you don't choose to take time to renew on our own. Burnout, depression, and illness are signs you have pushed yourself too hard.

Additionally, the more noise in your brain based on frustration and worry, the less your capacity to think, learn, and create.

The brain is not limitless. Short-term memory is finite. The container can only hold and process a certain amount of input. The more your brain needs to think about what has happened or will happen soon, the less productive you can be.

You also have external distractions overloading your circuits. Email, constant cell phone use, crowded spaces, and traffic create a constant level of anxiety that affects your learning and cognition. Neurons misfire, misalign, and fail to activate. You don't see details or hear everything said to you. In short, your brain runs out of space and gas.

On the other hand, happiness clears the mind of internal noise, freeing up space to think. It is easier to focus your attention. You more soundly evaluate options and consequences. You have a better sense of who you are and what you are doing. **You act in the Optimal Productive State**.

So why isn't happiness ever a factor in strategic plans?

Most companies still operate with threat and reward systems where *constructive feedback* is used more to motivate action instead of praise, encouragement, and collaborative creation. Leaders don't trust the power of positive emotions. They believe stress is good, that they make better decisions when the pressure is on. They don't realize what they lose to stress.

Some progressive companies recognize the need for employees to take breaks and have some fun. Yet, fun isn't the only emotion needed to create the Optimal Productive State. The emotions that enhance creativity and peak performance are those that make you *feel good*, which could be anything from feeling calm to giddy, from reassured to passionate, from reverent to mischievous. You have a range of emotional possibilities to choose from under the category of happiness. It's time to put activating personal joy into strategic planning and infuse corporate cultures with play, delight, and hope so everyone can do their best work.

Activating Choice

I found an enormous amount of research in sports psychology on how to master the art of being present. For an athlete to be a champion, he or she must know how to *step into the zone* where they do not think about anything, not even winning, to perform at their best. Thinking of winning causes their brains to entertain losing. Instead, they allow their bodies to express how good it feels to be doing what they love.

After interviewing top professional athletes in basketball, baseball, football, swimming, tennis, and golf, I found some similarities in the techniques they used to get into the zone. Some had unique and quirky superstitions, but they all used breathing, centering, and emotions to shift into the clarity and freedom they needed to be victorious.

I found the techniques used by these athletes help me remain present to my life. Any time I catch myself contemplating the past, fearing the future, or worrying about how others are judging me, I can deliberately alter my state of mind by practicing the four steps listed below. Whether warming up for a competition or a difficult conversation, you need to bring your brain and body into harmony before you make your next move.

The four steps include:

1. **Relax** your body.
2. **Detach** from the thoughts running in your head.

3. Bring the **Center** of your body into your awareness.
4. **Focus** on the emotion you want to feel.

Use these four steps to bring yourself back into alignment the moment you recognize symptoms of stress in your body, or as an adjustment before you address a group, engage in a conversation, or start a task or sport. You can practice the steps as a ritual to center yourself before the day begins and at night to help you sleep. You can Relax-Detach-Center-Focus any time to ensure you are savoring the moment, not missing a second of your life.

Step 1. Relax

Begin by relaxing your body. In the last section, you learned that stress directs blood flow away from the brain. Your emotional states show up in your body. Your muscles tighten, your breathing stops or slows down, your jaw clenches, your stomach churls, your arms and legs prepare you to fight or flight, and your shoulders droop. You might even find your fingers and toes curl up.

> You must release the tension in
> your body before you can clear your
> mind and shift your emotions.

Telling yourself to calm down only helps for a few seconds at a time. You must actively shift your biological state before you can control what is going on in your brain.

The first step is to focus on your breath. When stressed, you stop or shorten your breathing. Oxygen helps return your body to a state of harmony quicker than any thought or activity. Let your breathing return to a normal, easy rhythm.

Next, stimulate your blood flow by releasing the tension in your neck, back, arms, and legs. If you know where you tend to hold tension, go there. Breathe in and relax those spots. If you aren't sure where to focus, do a quick body *scan and release*. Start with your forehead and jaw, then move down your body. Repeat this mental scan and release your tension at various times throughout the day. You will have more energy when you need it.

My favorite release is to find something to laugh about. If you make finding the lighter side of life a daily discipline, your body will naturally relax.

Seeing the funny side of situations
turns drudgery into amusement.
Life literally lightens up.

Even if you want to stay angry, you first need to relax your body. You want to make it your conscious choice, not letting your brain choose for you.

To sustain relaxation, regularly engage in activities that release your brain and tension when you aren't working. Try meditation, yoga, or other calming practices. Participate in fun team sports. Do exercises you enjoy. Go dancing. Seek an activity that evokes pleasure and gratitude such as walking in the park or hiking in the desert, playing with your children or pets, or making time in your schedule for your favorite hobby.

You can also deliberately slow down your life. Eat more slowly, drive more leisurely, and walk at a gentler pace.

Before you can outsmart your brain, you must lighten up your body. The more you relax, the freer you are to choose.

Step 2. Detach

After you relax your body, free up the mind by detaching from the controlling chatter in your brain. Cleaning out the clutter—worries about work, money troubles, rough spots in relationships—makes space for possibilities.

The thoughts that most confuse and control you are the negative judgments you form about what you are perceiving. The Stoic philosopher Epictetus said nearly two thousand years ago, "Man is disturbed not by events that happen, but by his opinion of events that happen." The more energy you spend assessing a situation, the less you can observe all that is going on.

Of equal weight are concerns about opinions others have of you. And yet, as my acting coach Gary Austin insisted, "It's none of your business what people think of you. It's your business to give 100 percent to what you are trying to accomplish. Every moment you think about what someone else is thinking, you are taking from your best performance."[3] You get a lot more done when you quit taking everything so personally.

To control your mind, you first have to empty it.

You can see this phenomenon at work when you do something just for the fun of it. When you have nothing to lose, you're likely to do your best. You sink your longest putt, deliver a top-notch speech, and find the win-win solution.

> When you forget about the past and future—
> hopes, fears, needs, and expectations—
> you're free to plunge into the present.

In an interview during the 2000 Olympic Games in Sydney, champion sprinter Michael Johnson said that crossing the finish line feels great, but the real thrill comes at the start of the race. He said he did his best to be in "the here and now" with no thoughts about end results or competitors. When he ran, he didn't think about the passage of time. He felt the ease of his body moving and the rush of cool air on his skin. "The challenge," Johnson said, "is to maintain this presence until the experience is over and it's time to celebrate."

Once you can relax your body and detach from your thoughts, you can experience the present more completely. When you are free of the need to be liked, appreciated, and right, you'll see people in a new light. When you empty your mind, you can open your heart.

Start your practice of detaching by stopping your thoughts for one minute while observing the world around you. If your mind drifts off or you start judging, analyzing, or evaluating, let your thoughts float away. Return to noticing the details of the world around you for sixty seconds.

Tomorrow, increase your practice to two minutes. Each day, see how much longer you can go before your brain fills up with thoughts.

Here are four tips for helping you to detach:

Detaching Tip #1. Focus on what you can control.

Your brain likes to churn about things out of your control. The more time you spend talking, reading, worrying, and complaining about things out of your control, the more you fall into being a victim. Grousing about the work styles of others, the economy, your nosy neighbors, and why things can't be the way they used to be takes away from the time you can spend working on what you can do well right now. Focus instead on what you are able to control, like taking care of yourself, achieving the goals that excite you, and discovering a new way to get work done. This makes you powerful.

Detaching Tip #2. Let go of what you thought would happen.

Clinging to your expectations blocks out possibilities. We all have pictures of what we thought a situation, conversation, or meeting would look like. Then something else happened. If you aren't flexible, you will feel frustrated. Instead, choose to be present and go with the flow.

As they say in tennis, "Play the ball in front of you." If you choose to work with what you have, whether you like it or not, you may find you have enough to not only get by, but to keep moving forward.

Trust everything will work out. There is a possibility that the worst will happen. Just as strong is the possibility that the best will happen. You might not get what you want but the results could turn out to be better than you expected. Live with faith in possibility and more things will go right for you than wrong.

Detaching Tip #3. Walk lightly.

Taking your work and relationships seriously is admirable. Taking *yourself* too seriously is not. Woody Allen said, "Comedy is tragedy plus time." Laughter is a great time management tool.

Detaching Tip #4. Don't give up.

If you can't detach today, you may next time. You're teaching your brain a new trick. Letting go takes practice.

Step 3. Center

"Instincts never lie." "Trust your gut." "Listen to the voice deep inside you." These are some of the many sayings that point to a well of wisdom beyond your brain. Many Eastern philosophies teach the true center of the mind lies in the center of the body. To get there, you move your awareness out of your head and down into your core—an act known as centering.

Athletes, performers, and martial artists are taught to move their awareness to their diaphragm or a spot just below the navel. Some people focus on the area that fills with air in their belly. Some of my students tell me when they recall a moment in their life when they felt courageous, they feel a sense of warmth and strength from the center of their bodies. When you drop your awareness out of your head down past your heart, you will find your center, the point where you muster courage and the will to move forward.

To find your center, inhale deeply. Move your attention to the place below your navel where the breath fills your abdomen. While exhaling, keep your awareness on this spot. Let your awareness settle there for a minute as you become familiar with this part of yourself.

One way of releasing all thoughts so you can center your awareness is to imagine an elevator, or a lift as it is called in some parts of the world, in your brain. The doors are open but the elevator is empty. With eyes closed, watch each thought float toward and into the elevator. Once your thoughts are safely inside, the doors close. Then the elevator floats down from your brain, down your neck, your chest, and through the middle of your body. The elevator sets down at the bottom of your breath in your belly. The doors open but there is nothing inside but a warm glow that soothes your body. Once you feel calm and grounded, open your eyes but try to sustain the sensation of centering in your body.

Once a day, take a few moments to close your eyes, breathe deeply, and notice the center of your body. Keep your awareness here for as long as you can.

Once you are comfortable keeping your awareness out of your head and at your center, add a variety of activities to your practice. Play sports, read, listen to music, or hike while focusing your awareness on the center of your body. From this new perspective, you'll begin to see and hear more details and move with both strength and calmness.

Then you can take centering into your social interactions. Just the act of speaking and listening from your center builds rapport with others. They feel safer with you. They will hear what you say more clearly. The energy from your center adds a positive dynamic to your conversations.

Whenever you are having difficulty staying present, place one hand lightly on your tummy and tap your fingers. This brings your attention out of your head and into your body. Remind yourself to breathe.

As with all new habits, centering requires daily practice. Give yourself time to master it. Start your practice in nonthreatening situations. Stay consistent with your daily practice. Centering will become a habit instead of a technique.

Step 4. Focus

The fourth step, after relaxing, detaching, and centering is to choose one thought to anchor yourself to as you maintain yourself in the present. Thoughts have a way of sneaking into your brain no matter what you do. If you have one thought to anchor on, you can push the others away.

To outsmart your brain when your emotions have taken the wheel, choose the emotion you want to feel. You might consider how you want yourself and others to feel at the end of your interaction. Do you want people to feel hopeful, encouraged, curious, or proud? Then you need to feel the way you want others to feel while you are with them.

Before I speak to an audience or start a class, I consider what I want people to leave the room feeling. Sometimes I want them to feel happy, sometimes inspired, sometimes courageous, and sometimes eager to act. Whatever *emotional outcome* I want to create, I write the word on a piece of paper to set within my range of vision. If I get flustered during my presentation, I glance at my paper, I breathe in and feel the one emotion in my body. The right words then seem to show up.

When speaking one-on-one, I'll often focus on the words *care*, *love*, or *compassion* to help me remember that, above all, I want people to leave feeling that I care about them, I understand their experience, and I value our relationship even if we didn't agree.

Focusing on your emotions is also important when working alone. To intensify your concentration on a complex project, take a break and focus on how you want to feel when the work is done. You might choose *proud*, *excited*, or *grateful*. Pick an emotion and experience it, especially when you feel yourself drifting into stress. The emotional focus will keep you on track.

Staying in the Present

Standing in the present without thinking of the past or future can feel unnerving. It can also be magical. You might find you are wiser and more capable than you ever imagined. You will be amazed not only with the clarity and contentment you feel when you work in the present but also with the positive results when working with others.

When you Relax, Detach, Center, and Focus you will not only be more attuned to your inner world, you will also be more aware of the inner world of the people you are conversing with. You will find that often, all a person needs from you is to feel heard and they will be willing to listen to your brilliant ideas in return. Also, the energy from your emotional state can create a connection that activates optimism and creativity.

Staying in the present may take courage and patience. You may be trying to overcome a lifetime of distracting mental habits. To stay present with others, you need to notice when a judgment creeps in or if you are impatiently waiting to give your opinion. You can then choose to set aside your opinions to remain attentive. Trust you won't lose your good ideas; they will return to you if they were important.

The SET-C Method

The following method was created to give you steps to follow when trying to sort through the chatter in your mind. If you Relax-Detach-Center-and Focus quickly, you can make the best choices with what you know right now. If you find you are struggling to shift, that you are attached to an emotion you can't shake but it doesn't serve you in the end, these steps will help you move forward.

After you Relax-Detach-Center-and Focus, you can use the SET-C method to open your mind to options when working alone or with others, especially when you are with someone who seems stuck or resistant to change. Chapter 5 will take a deeper look at how to use the techniques you are learning to improve the outcomes of your interactions.

EXERCISE #3—The SET-C Method

The steps in the SET-C method include:

Tell the	**S**TORY
Identify the	**E**MOTION
Look for the	**T**RIGGER
Make your	**C**HOICE

TELL THE STORY. In your point of view, what is going on? Who or what would you like to blame? What details annoy you? What thoughts keep taking over? Be honest and don't try to edit the story you are telling.

IDENTIFY THE EMOTION. Name the emotions triggered by the situation. Check for tightness in your gut or jaw (anger?); shoulders, chest, and throat (fear?); bottom of your stomach (shame or embarrassment?); or heart (betrayal, disappointment, or sadness?). Look for more than one emotion. Anger could mask fear. You could feel happiness and envy at the same time. Use the inventory from your *Name That Emotion* exercise in Chapter 1.

LOOK FOR THE TRIGGER. What didn't you get that you really wanted? What did you want to happen or what did you expect to receive? What are you not getting from the situation that you need, such as respect, love, safety, or control? What do you fear losing, such as achievement, peace of mind, or autonomy? List ALL the reasons you might be feeling as you do. Remember, triggers are often not logical. You can decide if your reaction is worth acting on when you choose what to do next.

CHOOSE. Ask yourself, "Is it true someone is intentionally depriving me of my need?" If your answer is "yes", can you ask for what you need? If your answer is no, or you know for a fact that asking for what you need is a waste of time, can you let go of your need for now? Depending on your answers, choose how you now want to feel based on how you want this story to end.

For example, if you feel impatient because you know you are right in an argument, yet you admit that your partner is not trying to make you look stupid, you might choose to acknowledge that there are many ways to view a situation with two of those viewpoints in the room. If you feel a colleague betrayed you by sharing your idea with someone else, then you can choose to tell the person how you feel and ask him or her to remain silent in the future, or you can choose to share your secrets with more trusting friends. Choose your health and well-being over taxing your nervous and immune systems as often as you can.

For the next week, during or after difficult conversations, use the SET-C method to explore your options. To achieve your outcome, choose to:

- Ask for what you need or let it go.
- Choose to focus on an emotion that will help you get the outcome you think is possible. If you need to let go and move on, consider how humor, gratitude, or compassion could help.

Although the SET-C method is a good reflective technique, you will see amazing results if you can learn to use it under duress. When you feel stress, frustration, anxiety, or anger, the quicker you identify the trigger and choose your emotion and next action, the sooner you will decrease your stress and limit behavior you might regret. Use the SET-C method to activate your free will.

■ *Practical Tips*

1. Consider using RELAX—DETACH—CENTER—FOCUS:

   a. as you are walking to your office or work station to align yourself with your goals and intentions for the day;

   b. before conversations, including phone calls, to increase your ability to listen;

   c. the moment you catch yourself arguing or shutting down during a conversation or meeting;

   d. when you are ending a conversation to make sure you feel a sense of completion on all issues; or

   e. at the end of your work day so that you leave issues at work to help make your evening relaxing and enjoyable.

2. In the heat of the moment remember to RELAX—DETACH—CENTER—FOCUS before using your SET-C Method to more easily discover a path to resolution or a way forward.

"Realize that now, in this moment of time, you are creating. You are creating your next moment. That is what's real."
—Sara Paddison, *The Hidden Power of the Heart*

.

CHAPTER 4
REMOVING THE ROADBLOCKS TO SUCCESS

Making Space for Personal Work

The author and former Secretary of Health, Education, and Welfare, John W. Gardner said, "Human beings have always employed an enormous amount of clever devices for running away from themselves. We keep ourselves busy, fill our lives with so many diversions, stuff our heads with so much knowledge, involve ourselves with so many people, and cover so much ground that we never have time to probe the fearful and wonderful world within. By middle life, most of us are accomplished fugitives from ourselves."

Personal computers were supposed to give us endless leisure time. The opposite happened. Life gets busier every year.

How many times a day do you find yourself facing a colleague, friend, or family member who is speaking to you, and you haven't a clue what they are saying? You smile, nod, say "uh-huh" and "hmm," and wonder how many emails you have waiting for you, what tasks you still have to do, and what you will say when the person finally takes a breath. When on the phone, you answer your email, plan your weekend activities, and edit the report that is past due. Then you are annoyed because the person you are conversing with doesn't understand your point of view.

To act with emotional intelligence—to be both self-aware and able to determine what is at the source of the thoughts and behavior of others—you must be present to the moment. Staying present to the moment means keeping our mind fully engaged with what is happening in the space you are occupying. It is a difficult skill to master. No matter how mindful you try to be, worries and unfinished work creep into the crevices of your brain, pulling you away.

In fact, you are probably a master at being anywhere else but in the present moment. You can zone out practically anywhere and still survive. Where is your mind while you are driving? How often do you realize you haven't been thinking about driving for miles? How many other drivers do you suppose are operating on automatic pilot? Think about these questions the next time you refuse to fasten your seat belt.

Added to your too-hectic life is your propensity to multitask. When you multitask, you are only partially attentive to each task you are doing. This causes you to miss important details, annoy people you are with, and lose track of priorities.

On the other hand, you can give 100 percent of your attention to a task and still not be effective. Notice what is going on in your mind and body the next time you stand up after sitting at the computer for over an hour. Do you feel drained or energized? Do you feel ready to take on the next task or would you prefer a break, maybe even a neck massage? When you focus on one thing for too long, you can lose perspective. It's hard to move on to do something else, including answering emails and phone calls which can cause misunderstandings and hurt feelings when you can't shift your focus. And, you tend to lose your sense of humor. Overfocusing is not fun.

> It's time you learn how to corral your
> mind into paying attention to the
> world going on in front of you.

I first learned how to *tune into the present* by accident. One morning, I turned on the computer even though I knew a client would be calling me in five minutes. I promised myself I would not read my email. I was curious to see what messages were waiting for a reply. My cat, PK, crawled into my lap.

My screen quickly filled with new email. I mumbled about the lack of time, the shackle of work I had created, and the people who had nothing better to do than chatter on social media. While reading the list, PK began one of her long cat-stretches. After extending a leg toward the ceiling, she slowly lowered it to the keyboard, resting her paw on the "Delete" key. I watched in horror as, one by one, my messages disappeared. I stared at a blank screen.

Following my panic, I decided the only thing I could do was to clear my mind as she had cleared my screen. I turned off the computer, made myself a cup of tea, and curled up on the couch with the phone.

I had a fabulous coaching session with my client. I detected more meaning in her words, her tone, and her silences than I had in previous discussions. My observations were more evocative and my questions had more impact. She declared me a wizard among coaches. I didn't tell her that I had just had a session from a far better coach than me—my cat.

So how do you train your brain to be in the present moment? Doing the exercises in this chapter will help you overcome your mental conditioning and alter your life to support your ability to outsmart your brain. You will be creating new habits. This takes discipline, persistence, and practice, but the return on your investment is worth it.

With renewed energy, confidence, and consciousness, you increase your ability to objectively assess your emotional reactions. These habits will give you the mental clarity to freely choose how to feel and think as soon as possible after your brain has reacted to a situation.

Fortifying Your Personal Foundation

Your physical energy and mental preoccupation affect your ability to act with emotional intelligence. Feeling tired, hungry, overweight, overwhelmed, worried about money, unsure about relationships and your future, and guilty about your action or inaction will increase the intensity of your emotional reactions. You will find it more difficult to remember to shift your emotions. You lose access to your choices. Therefore, enhancing your well-being and decreasing your stress increases your ability to act intelligently.

Fortunately, many books and seminars are available to teach you techniques for building your confidence and decrease your stress. To help you implement these techniques and fortify your personal foundation, consider how you can:

- create a vision of how you want your life to look and feel;
- set your yearly theme and goals to move you toward your vision;
- regularly question if your assumptions, beliefs, and habits support your theme and goals; and
- hire a coach or join a group that will support you in making the life changes you need to stay on the path to realizing your vision.

Knowing where you are headed in life and committing to ongoing personal development supports your ability to recognize your emotional triggers and make good decisions. Then you want to limit stress to stay attentive to what is going on in the present.

You must take care of yourself so that you can stay alert to your thinking. The less stressed you are, the more you can intelligently analyze what is going on in your brain and consider different options for how you might respond.

If you don't make this commitment, the exercises in this book will be difficult to repeat over time. It's tough enough staying present with all the external noises and demands on your time. Then you have your chatty brain well-trained to deceive you. As you learned in Chapter 2, the brain's primary function is to protect you. It is always on the lookout for attackers. Therefore, the brain tends to see the world in a negative frame. It's difficult to stay optimistic and happy with a brain that is biologically trained to be defensive.

Therefore, it takes a lot of energy to outsmart your brain. You need a healthy and alert mental state to get to the core of what is *really* activating your emotional reactions so you can better resolve problems and discover more meaningful solutions. To increase your stamina, complete the **Self-Care Checklist in Appendix B**. Raise your score and you increase your capacity to outsmart your brain.

> If you desire to increase your ability to access emotional intelligence, you must commit to decreasing your stress. This is lifelong work, not a one-time event.

If I Only Had the Nerve…Cultivating Confidence

Doing things well is an important factor in achieving goals. You also need to have a good sense of "who you are" beyond your skills and knowledge to stay determined and resilient in difficult times. Are you smart, compassionate, and bold? Are you generous, patient, and attentive? Do you have a sense of humor, an open mind, and a thirsty curiosity? Know your strengths and honor them. These traits are the treasures of life that no one can take away from you.

The following exercise will give you a sense of who you are. If you want to further develop your confidence, you might work with a counselor or personal coach to strengthen your sense of self.

I had a difficult adolescence. I ended my teenage years spending my twentieth birthday in jail. Thankfully, one of my cellmates taught me that I was not the sum of my actions. Instead, I was the total of my powers. On a dreary day when I was lost in self-pity reflecting on the life I thought I had ruined, she pushed me against the wall and said, "You have no idea who you are. You are smart, you are strong, and for some reason, you care deeply about people. When you get that in here (she pointed to my heart), you will get out of here."

My life had been focused on achievement. I had to do well in school, excel in sports, and master whatever activity I tried. This was the first time someone made me look at *who* I was outside of what I do. I didn't need to excel at doing to be worthwhile as a human being. My cellmate saved my life.

With a fresh understanding of *who* I was, I found a sense of purpose. When I was released, I pushed through temptation and overcame my drug addiction. Three years later, I graduated summa cum laude and went on to build a successful and satisfying life. Without claiming my powers, I may have given up.

Of course, life hasn't been simple. Knowing *who I am* continues to give me the strength to work through the snags and disappointments. I also regularly work on myself. Studying and teaching emotional intelligence and coaching skills fortifies my awareness and growth.

The first step is to identify the strengths that make up who you are. These attributes will differ from person to person. Your list of traits may match or differ from mine.

Then, to build your confidence, the next step is to go beyond *knowing* your strengths. You must claim them for yourself. If you are asked about your talents and gifts, you won't be embarrassed to mention them. When you walk proudly with your strengths, you are better able to speak from your heart and gut.

Who you are is not the same thing as the descriptions you offer when you introduce yourself at a party. When you say, "I'm a lawyer; I'm a progressive; I'm a mother of four; I'm a single parent; I'm a catholic; I'm a baby boomer; I'm an animal-lover," you are identifying a group you claim allegiance to. The labels define roles you play and indicate how you see the world. You can change these titles and corresponding actions anytime even if you think you can't. You can choose what you do and what groups you belong to as your experiences and views change. In fact, you should regularly question and evaluate the labels you identify with throughout your life. Use the SET-C method to determine if your choices are right for you as your life and needs evolve.

Your skills and knowledge also do not define who you are; they just show you what you can do right now. Instead, look at what it took to gain the skills, knowledge, and wisdom you now have. You can use these strengths to add to your skills and knowledge, or you can seek new skills and knowledge if you feel it's time to make a change.

EXERCISE #4—Know Your Powers

STEP #1—Recall a peak experience where you felt fully alive and fulfilled.

A time where you overcame a major challenge in your life.

At the completion of an important project or personal goal.

A time you were working hard to achieve a goal on your own or inspiring others to give their all to achieve the goal.

Go back to this moment and recall how good you felt about yourself when you accomplished this.

STEP #2—List at least five character traits you possess that you called on to create this peak experience. Consider your:

- Internal Strengths and Gifts
- Strong Emotions and Attitude
- Personal Values
- Unique Sense/Perspective

This list represents the part of you that makes you great even more than your accomplishments. Choose from items such as:

PICK YOUR POWERS

Courage • Conviction • Commitment • Calmness under pressure • Love of life • Love for people • Love of self • Confidence • Sense of humor • Playfulness • Flexibility •

Decisiveness • Determination • Integrity • Ability to admit vulnerability • Grace • Sensitivity • Generosity • Loyalty • Honesty • Enthusiasm • Appreciation • Faith • Joyfulness • Peacefulness • Patience • Curiosity • Daring • Openmindedness • Willingness to learn • Creativity • Empathy • Care • Compassion • Ability to receive • Appreciation of differences • Unconditional respect • Responsibility • Courage to show love • Positive energy • Trust • Kindness.

The list is not complete; use your own words to describe what you can claim that makes you great. The items on your list add up to the total of your Personal Power, how capable you are of shaping your future.

The use of power in this context refers only to the strengths you own that cannot be taken away. Money, titles, and possessions may give you power, yet they can disappear in a day. Good looks reap rewards, yet the ravages of time, accidents, and illness pick away at surface beauty. Mastering the fear of aging is a far greater triumph than using technology to stay one step ahead of nature. Growing old is a privilege not everyone gets. Even your skills—how well you speak, hunt, cook, handle finances, teach, write, or problem solve—can be lost by time or stolen by circumstance.

In her book, *The Last Word on Power,* Tracy Goss explains the power needed to make the impossible happen. She says it has nothing to do with authority or competence. Goss said, "When you acquire this power, you can operate with a quality and integrity that frees you to take the risks and actions necessary to change the world."[1]

The secret formula for your own success is the composite of who you are. No single characteristic ensures victory. Talented people lose, courageous people fall, and smart people fail. It is the sum of the elements that determines the amplitude of your power. You must discover and claim *your* strengths so you can proudly exploit them to transform the world around you.

Also, be willing to declare your limitations. If you acknowledge that sometimes you lie, you gossip, you are insensitive, impatient, judgmental, and rude, then you are more likely to notice when you might repeat these behaviors. Then, using the techniques you are learning in this book, you can shift how you feel and do something else. Relax, detach, center, and focus, and then use your SET-C steps to reflect on your mind-set and options. Admitting your limitations doesn't strengthen them; admitting you are human gives you the freedom to choose how you want to show up in life. When you bring your limitations to light, they lose power. You are then free to choose what to feel and do next.

Finally, consider the difference between confidence and arrogance as you assess your self-assurance. Confidence means you rely on yourself. Arrogance requires you to compare yourself to others.

When your confidence is solid, you do not have to win or be right to feel good about yourself. Winning and perfection are not prerequisites for confidence. Whereas arrogance leaves no margin for error, confidence keeps you from labeling mistakes or losses as failures. Mistakes, though you might feel embarrassed or angry, are just indications that there is more to learn. Losses, though you might feel sad or frustrated, indicate the need to alter your actions or expectations. Fear can coexist with confidence. Arrogant people don't like admitting they have fears; confident people are willing to admit they have fears and have the courage to ask for help when they do. They trust that there is a way to move forward despite their fears.

Arrogance adds a feeling of superiority to the measure. They see people as being either more than or less than they judge themselves to be. To feel good, arrogant people find fault in others to prop themselves up. When they fail, they blame others. When they make mistakes, they beat themselves up. This constant comparing and belittling drains the joy from relationships and activities. Triumph produces righteousness, even indignation.

When you focus on giving a voice to your powers, you work on your confidence. Other people might do better than you; this doesn't take away from your potential. You don't need to find fault in others to know what you can achieve. You can better master your brain when you feel powerful and confident.

The Company You Keep

To assist your growth, surround yourself with people as much as you can who are committed to strengthening their personal foundations. If you spend time with people who consider self-care as vital and who have a strong personal vision, it will be easier to stay on your own developmental path. Additionally, look for people who keep stress at a minimum, who know and honor their priorities in work and life, who admit to not being perfect, and who are confident enough to ask for what they need. Use this criterion for selecting friends, life partners, and when hiring colleagues. Your emotions and choices reflect the company you keep.

Ultimately, if everyone practiced self-care, self-awareness, and conscious choice, and then chose to develop their confidence, empathy, and compassion, we might create more emotionally intelligent cultures and communities. Organizations should list confidence, adaptability, patience, and emotional awareness as equal in importance to technical knowledge and skills if they want to increase the bottom line. When employees have good emotional intelligence and strong personal foundations, the health of the organization will provide a strong return on the investment.

Three Elements of Change

If you are taking care of the stress in your life, strengthening your confidence, and noticing the world around you in the present, there will still be times your emotions take the wheel. You can't stop your emotions from being triggered, but you can choose what to do next. Sometimes this will be easy. When it's not easy, reflect on these three areas to determine what is getting in the way of change:

- Willingness
- Desire
- Courage

1. You must be **willing** to do what it takes to change;
2. the change must provide a payoff you **desire;** and
3. you must have the **courage** to ask for what you want or to let go of your attachments,

If one of these factors is missing, you may fall victim to your resistance to change. Explore each of these conditions when you feel resistance. You might find what you need to change your mind.

Willingness

An old riddle asks, "If three frogs are basking in the sun on a lily pad and one decides to jump, how many frogs are left behind?" The answer is three. Deciding to jump is not the same as jumping.

Here is another riddle, "If three people sitting around a table are complaining about a coworker's behavior and one decides it's time to address the problem, how many people are left sitting at the table?" Yes, three.

Before you will open your mind to see a situation in a new light and then act on a decision, you need:

1. the willingness to accept evidence that your assumptions about a person/situation may or may not be true; and
2. the willingness to stop reacting and do something else.

What does it take to be willing?

Unfortunately, it often takes a crisis before you are willing to accept that how you judge a situation or person might be inaccurate. Sometimes, you may be aware of the holes in your thinking, yet you still don't accept responsibility for improving the situation. Instead, you rationalize your perspective and assumptions, and then justify your judgments. What makes it so hard to be willing?

Remember that the reactive and social centers of your brain first want to protect you. Iyanla Vanzant wrote in *One Day My Soul Just Opened Up*, "I was not willing to make people angry or hurt their feelings... I was not willing to sound weird or stupid or like a know-it-all. I was not willing to run the risk of being wrong. I was not willing or prepared to defend myself if I were challenged. Yes, I admit it. I knew what needed to be done, but I was not willing to do it."[2]

Fears and attachments to anger over the needs you wanted but were not met hold you captive, yet acknowledging them diffuses their power. Anger over receiving a negative evaluation can be overcome when you accept that some people will *never* like what you do or say. The fear of being wrong is surmountable when you admit you can't know everything and no one likes to be around people who talk as if they do. Declaring your fear or irritation out loud takes the air out of the emotion.

When you are willing to admit you are envious of someone, and you're afraid that you may never reach the same level of success as they, you can soften your envy and fear. You can admit you actually admire the accomplishments of the person regardless of your jealousy. You can acknowledge what you're willing to do to feel prouder of yourself, and what you don't want to do. You're free to do what is in your best interest based on your values and desires even though the envy still exists.

To support your willingness to see, speak, or act differently, seek out people whom you trust to explore the rut of emotion you are stuck in. Make sure you find people who want to discover what is making them stuck as well. You can also hire a coach who will take a stand for your highest potential. The greater the discomfort you feel in your relationships at home or at work, the more vital it is to have at least one person you can share your story with and explore the triggers together.

Be careful of your well-thought-out excuses when telling your story. Yes, you need your paycheck. You would rather not offend your boss. You have too much to do than to sit down and have a talk with a colleague that could result in a waste of time. What else is true is that you don't have the time to let the poison of ongoing emotions course deeper. You don't have the stamina to suppress all your negative emotions without affecting your health and your ability to be happy. At work, you don't have enough margin in your bottom line to let your emotions erode productivity. Are you willing to do what it takes to make the positive change? You must answer yes before you can do the work.

> It's time to declare your willingness to look at your beliefs and assumptions, to bring your fears to light, and to give voice to your desires.

Willingness is the first door that leads to mental clarity. If you are willing to be honest with yourself and others, and to let them be honest with you in return, you've taken a giant leap toward better relationships and long-term solutions.

EXERCISE #5—Test Your Willingness
The purpose of this exercise is to help you recognize what it feels like in your body when you are unwilling to change your emotions and thoughts.

You must know what unwillingness feels like to recognize its existence.

To complete the exercise, you need a pen, paper, and a timer. You can do this alone or with a partner.

1. **List three beliefs that are important to you but do not make a big difference in the world.** For example, does it irritate you when people put the toilet paper roll on the wrong way? Do the dishes need to be washed immediately and not sit in the sink for a while? Should people return what they borrow to the place where they found it? Should clothing be folded a certain way? Is being on time always important? Should people at work smile or somehow acknowledge you when you pass them in the hallway? Come up with three of your own pet peeves. Make sure they are small in the big scheme of life and that the action you don't like isn't against the law or a safety hazard.

2. **Pick one of your beliefs.** Set your timer for one minute. Spend the next sixty seconds quickly finding all the reasons why this one belief may not be true. Argue against yourself. Be creative, even silly. Discover how the action you don't like could be positive for someone else. However, DO NOT TAKE ON THE ROLE OF SOMEONE ELSE, such as your spouse or your friend. You must come up with your own

reasons and arguments, no matter how much you do not believe in them. You can have your original belief back after you play the game for a minute. If you have a partner, have this person argue for your belief while you argue against it. This is more difficult and more effective.

3. **Ask yourself these questions.** What did it feel like when you had to argue against your belief? What did it take for you to be willing to argue against yourself? Could you feel the resistance in your stomach or in your throat? What did you learn about yourself when you attached to your belief? How hard was it to let go? If you did let go, what did it take? If the exercise was difficult, repeat steps 1–3 again with another belief from your list.

4. **Apply what you learned to your life.** For example, imagine working on a project where you have a belief about how it should be done differently from the way it is being handled. Are you able to let go of your belief about how it should be done? What beliefs are causing rifts in your relationships? What about inevitable changes—if you have been resisting and complaining about an impending change, can you find good reasons to accept what will take place? Where do your beliefs have you trapped? Do you avoid people for reasons that happened a long time ago? Do you complain

about meetings being a waste of time instead of trying to make them more productive? Do you stick to your ways of doing things no matter what? Can you argue against yourself, breaking your paradigms to allow for change and growth? The answers to these questions will give you a peek at your willingness, and unwillingness, to change.

Once you begin to loosen your blocks, you will begin to recognize when other people are so attached to their beliefs that they are blinded to possibilities. Instead of telling them to change, see if they will explore the beliefs they are attached to. Then you can ask if they would be willing to see the situation a different way. Don't make them wrong. Make them right from their point of view, then see if they would be willing to see your perspective so you can find common ground.

> Don't put a lot of energy into holding
> onto ideas that make no difference
> in the big scheme of things.

Willingness is essential to resolving problems and strengthening your relationships. Can you step out of your frame, out of "the world according to you" for the chance of improving communications and results? If you do, you might find no good reasons to change your mind. Or you might find many.

To help you judge how quickly you bounce back from disappointment and frustration, take the **Find Your Resiliency Rate** quiz in Appendix C. Then you can make a plan to strengthen your agility and adaptability.

Desire

The second element in the formula for change is "desire." You may be *willing* to work on new solutions, take a risk, make a change, or listen to a different point of view. Unless there is a payoff based on something you want, your willingness may not last long.

Willingness is short-term. It opens the door to possibility, but makes no promises. Willingness is a cognitive decision made for the moment. You say, "I'll try" but have not yet committed to the change. You say things like, "I'll try to quit smoking," "I'll try to stay calm and listen," "I'll try to do my best" as a first step. To take the next step in changing perspective and behavior, you must have a strong desire to make the change last over time.

In other words, talk is cheap. If you listen to someone else's point of view only because you think it's the right thing to do, or you try to break a habit to please someone else, you will soon revert to your old ways of thinking and behaving. You must want to change for yourself before you are capable of really listening and breaking old habits. Willingness is a cognitive decision; desire is an emotion.

> You don't change because you should. Logic
> may initiate change, but it cannot sustain it
> without the emotional support of desire.

Without heartfelt desire, it's easier to find a rationalization than to take responsibility for your actions. The essayist Hannah Moore wrote in 1881, "The ingenuity of self-deception is inexhaustible." You can count on bad timing, your self-centered manager, clueless people, your dysfunctional upbringing, or your overwhelming responsibilities to give you reasons for not changing.

To create desire, you must first accept that you have a say about the outcome even in the most difficult situation. You are at least responsible for how you feel now and in the future. In accepting yourself as personally powerful, you can begin to acknowledge your desires. What would your life look like if you were in control? How free would you feel if you lived your life by choice? How badly do you want this for yourself? Even choosing to do nothing for a time is more powerful than waiting for others to act.

Once you determine you are willing to try to make a change, you need to find the payoff that will fuel your desire. Payoffs that inspire change are usually related to something you value such as having more money, love, peace, adventure, achievement, balance, recognition, or success. If you see that changing your outlook or behavior might lead to something you value, you are more apt to be open to new possibilities.

The following list includes some of the things most valued in life. Choose those items that you feel are critical to your happiness. Then, when you face a challenge, see if you can tie improving the situation to one of your values.

Values That Fuel Desire

Achievement: *Successful completion of visible tasks and projects*

Advancement: *Getting ahead, aspiring to higher levels*

Adventure: *Challenge, risk-taking, testing limits*

Aesthetics: *Desire for beautiful surroundings, artistic expression*

Challenge: *Testing physical or mental limits*

Community: *Neighbors or coworkers are familiar, friendly, and helpful*

Competence: *Being good at what you do, capable, effective*

Creativity: *Finding new ways to do things, composing, discovering*

Environment: *Respecting the earth and living in safe, comfortable spaces*

Fairness: *Respecting everyone's rights*

Family: *Taking care of and spending time with relatives*

Freedom: *Ability to make one's own decisions and choices*

Friendship: *Close companionship, ongoing and supportive relationships*

Health: *Maintain and enhance physical well-being*

Helping: *Taking care of others, assisting others to flourish*

Honesty: *Sincere, truthful, keeping promises*

Humor: *Fun, lightness, spontaneity*

Inner Harmony: *Freedom from inner conflict, integrated, whole*

Integrity: *Acting in line with beliefs, doing what you said you would*

Independence: *Self-reliance, autonomy*

Intellectual: *Learning about and discussing an area of knowledge*

Intimacy: *Deep connection with others*

Neatness: *Tidy, orderly, clean, easy to work with*

Peace: *Harmony among people and groups*

Perseverance: *Pushing through to the end, completing tasks and goals*

Personal Growth: *Continual learning and personal development*

Pleasure: *Personal satisfaction, enjoyment, delight*

Position: *Being highly regarded in one's social group*

Power: *Having the authority/ability to direct events, make things happen*

Prosperity: *Flourishing, well-off, easily obtaining desires*

Security: *Freedom from worry, safe from threats*

Spirituality: *Deep connection with one's faith, belief in the divine*

Stability: *Certainty, predictability*

Teamwork: *Cooperating with others toward a common goal*

Tradition: *Respecting the way things have been done in the past*

Winning: *Successful when competing, coming out on top*

Your values will differ from other people. Do not assume what you value will match those of your colleagues or even those of your spouse. You can determine what they most value by asking them. Only then can you work together to find solutions that honor the values and desires of everyone involved.

Also, values can change in priority over time. As I grow older, I hold more value for activities that improve my health. Since I have no children and my parents have passed away, my value for family has weakened and my value for friendship has increased. These days, my passion for learning is greater than the desire for winning that drove me in my twenties and thirties. Events, age, and wisdom will change your perspective on what you hold most dear.

At work, levels of performance depend on the perception of a valued payoff. If you want people to work more efficiently or with more effort, you must find out and align your expectations to their greatest values. For example, you might link the work goals to the person's desire to make a difference, to their pride of achievement, to their love of adventure, or to a benefit for their family. Linking work goals to personal values ignites the fires of internal motivation.

EXERCISE #6—Test Your Desire

To help you judge how much energy you will put into completing a goal, assess if the obligation is tied to what you desire. The next time you are asked to do something, stop and complete these three steps:

1. **HESITATE.** Before you say "yes" to one more project, make a promise to a friend, or declare a personal goal, take a deep breath.

2. **ASSESS** your motivation. Ask yourself, "Do I really want to do this?" If you aren't sure, try to envision yourself carrying out your commitment. Does it make you feel good? Be careful not to take on assignments out of guilt or because you feel you should.

3. **DISCOVER.** If you feel you need to take on the task or meet the challenge, look at your list of values. Can you relate the outcome to something you value? Desire must be present to make a full-hearted commitment. You need to tie the change you want to make or the goal you want to achieve to a strong desire if you hope to weather the storms. Too many failures can be explained by these five words, "my heart wasn't in it."

Courage

One of the reasons I became a leadership coach was to be able to work with people over time to help them realize their visions. As a trainer, I saw thousands of people leave my classes ready to try out their new skills and ideas. Yet, the enthusiasm rarely lasted for more than a day. Once faced with a conflict that pushed their buttons or a task they preferred not to do, the good intentions flew out the window.

Yes, they were willing to try new techniques...to a degree. Yes, they desired better results...to a point. As soon as they faced their discomfort or doubt, they forgot their promises and returned to their old behaviors. They knew what they should do and didn't do it. The protective brain once again silenced their hearts.

It takes courage to take risks if failure is a real possibility. It takes bravery to say things differently if people might think something is wrong with you. It's easier to say "no" to yourself than to persist.

> Rationalizing and defending your behavior
> keeps you nestled in a safe, mediocre, and
> suffocating world. Mustering the courage to say,
> "Yes!" in the face of possible embarrassment
> or loss is a great gift to give yourself.

Improvisational actors are taught to say "yes" to keep a scene moving. They practice going with the flow and engaging with what shows up.

Life is the ultimate improvisational stage. You need courage to step into the moment with both feet.

Success often requires you muster the courage to act without a clear picture of the outcome. If you say, "I want to change, just not today," you'll miss your chance.

What gives rise to the courage to act? Joseph Campbell said we all have the chance to be heroes in our lives, to stand strong before monsters. When faced with a challenge, heroes clear their minds and cast out the urge to resist, fight, or flee. When their minds are clear, they can access their greatest weapon—instinctual consciousness, or wisdom.[3]

Whenever you choose to do something when your mind is saying, "No," you are acting as a hero. You are facing your fear and choosing to do what you *feel is right* from your heart and gut. This requires you to relax, detach, center, and focus on 1) the outcome you want to create, and 2) how you want to feel when you walk away from the situation.

Standing strong in the present moment allows you to go into your heart and gut to listen for answers. Sometimes I take a deep breath, clear my mind, tap my heart, and focus on my vision to help me figure out how I want to spend my day. Then, I courageously punch in the phone number, get a commitment to meet for a conversation, start my next book, throw out old stuff, or take the first step in creating the next chapter of my life.

When you act with courage to fulfill your values and desires, if things don't work out, you know you gave it your best shot. With your values and vision in mind, declare your willingness, claim your desires, and boldly leap forward with courage.

■ *Practical Tips*

1. Complete your Self-Care Checklist and set goals to increase your score.

2. Make a list of your top ten Personal Powers. Stand up and say, "I am…" as you confidently read your list. Do this before you make a presentation or start a conversation so you stay alert to the choices you have to feel, speak, and act.

3. At the end of the day, write down issues that feel unresolved or situations that turned out differently than you had hoped for. Determine if you:

    a. were not willing to see possibilities;

    b. didn't have a payoff for pursuing a better resolution; or

    c. lacked the courage to change your perspective or to act.

Then decide what you need to do next.

4. When you aren't sure of what your next steps should be in a situation, use your Presence Routine to RELAX—DETACH—CENTER—FOCUS, then ask your heart or your gut what to do. The wisdom in your body is often more reliable than the thoughts in your head.

"In the beginning, people were expressing fixed positions, which they were tending to defend, but later it became clear that to maintain the feeling of friendship in the group was more important than to maintain any position…
A new kind of mind begins to come into being."
—David Bohm, *On Dialogue*

CHAPTER 5
MAKING POWERFUL CONNECTIONS

Personal Mastery Expands Empathy

You now know that your brain is always on the lookout for an enemy that can harm you. The vigilance goes beyond physical harm to being alert to attacks on your personal needs that define and are important to you, such as your desires to be respected, heard, and acknowledged.

Any event, conversation, or how someone looks at you can trigger an emotion, even if the reaction is relief. The trigger activates a biochemical reaction. If you notice the effect on your body, your conscious brain gives a label to the reaction. The label is what you call "a feeling." If you then judge the emotional state as negative, your brain may choose to suppress it, keeping you from acknowledging the feeling. It takes willingness to look at and objectively assess the situation, desire to explore possibilities based on preferred outcomes, and the courage to act or let go to be able to access your power of choice.

A wonderful side effect of practicing emotional intelligence with your own reactions and choices, is the deepening of your capacity to empathise.

Influence

In addition to resolving conflicts, you can use the SET-C method to hear the desires and values of those you work with. If you can align the results you want with what people want for themselves, you have a greater chance of influencing their decisions.

When it comes to work, most people need to feel as if they are valued for their intelligence and ability. They also need to feel there is a payoff for their hard work and if they try to act or see things differently, they won't be punished if they make a mistake. They want to work for leaders who encourage them to take risks and to express how they feel about the present and future without penalty. They want their working environment to feel safe, where people respect each other even when they disagree.[1] They also want to know the meaning and value of their contributions, and to enjoy themselves as often as they can.

Each person has their own needs based on the emotional triggers you identified in Chapter 2. Needs vary by the individual and can shift in a lifetime. To know what people want and need, you need to ask them. Then, when you notice negative reactions in their faces, bodies, and words, you should consider what need is at the source of their reaction as you decide what to say and how to act in response.

Influencing people to see a different point of view or to behave in a different way requires you listen to their needs, values, and desires first. Only then can you have a conversation that will inspire a shift in perspective.

Listening requires you pay attention to the entire experience of the person you are speaking to with an attitude of curiosity.

Instead of pushing your point, acknowledge when someone is tense or uncomfortable. Instead of accepting words of agreement, probe deeper when the words don't match the pursed lips, lack of eye contact, or clenched fist. Instead of backing down when someone says they would rather not talk, sense what they need from you, such as attention, safety, appreciation, or love. Then see what you can offer that might open the door to further communication. If someone is not opening up to you, stop and ask yourself, "How am I listening?" You may need to shift your emotions and beliefs before they will trust speaking with you.

This requires you to, at the same time, continue to be alert to your own emotional reactions. I don't mean you become self-conscious. The skill is to notice if there is a shift in your body. Did your muscles tense up, your breathing shorten, or you felt the urge to look away? Once you notice your stomach clenched, your breathing stopped, or your head tilted, determine if you need to stop the conversation to ask for clarification or to share that you had a reaction to what was said. You might also realize that your reaction is not important, and that you need to relax and release the need to judge, argue, defend, or advise.

The quicker you choose to relax and shift, the sooner you can return to being attentive to others.

When I am coaching someone, my reactions are not important. I need to stay present to what they are offering with their words, their emotions, and the shifts in their tone and gestures. My values might differ from the person I am coaching, especially when I am in another country. I notice the reaction in my body and then exhale to release the tension. This clears my mind so I don't lose my ability to listen.

I was coaching a man in China who was contemplating being a coach after he retired from his HR leadership position in a big Chinese company. I asked him what he loved about his current job. He listed the many ways he developed people to realize their potential. He ended by saying, "And I love instilling the principles of Communism."

My body shuddered. His words challenged my deeply held value for Democracy, but I was coaching him, not teaching him. I breathed, sat up, and returned my attention to the man who loved helping others grow.

It's easy to get stuck in an emotional reaction because a situation or person does not conform to your view of how the world should be. Your brain defends threats to your identity and what you believe is right as if the speaker is personally attacking you. If your reactions go unchecked, you might do or say something that damages the relationship, sometimes for good. To maintain healthy, respectful, and comfortable relationships, you must accept that other people see the world and situations differently from you based on their past experiences, culture, upbringing, and values. There might be another point of view that is as feasible as yours for the world they live in.

> When you remove your blocks to seeing
> an event from another angle and the
> person in a different light, you can
> create something new together.

Your ability to catch your reactions is also helpful when you address groups or participate in meetings. For example, I was delivering one of my Leading with Emotional Intelligence speeches when a man in a military uniform loudly asked for permission to ask a question. I gladly complied. He challenged my statement that desire was a greater motivator than fear for improving productivity.

Instead of disagreeing with him, citing evidence of how fear restricts brain functions, I acknowledged his point of view. I said, "You're right. Fear can motivate. It pulls people together quickly when they feel under attack. We need your type of leadership when working with people in times of crisis." I watched as his body and face relaxed. Then I added, "And I'm hoping we don't see the need for creating war zones in the workplace. Few people can handle this type of motivation for very long."

A door opened; he was willing to listen even if he didn't completely agree. I explained how the expectation of performance, obedience, and quick results could kill creativity and innovation if there is no apparent crisis. When I asked if he could accept my answer, he said he was willing to see that fear could have both good and bad effects, depending on the requirements of the situation.

I had sensed his need to be right and maybe to win. It would have been a mistake for me to argue with him. I acknowledged him first, which invited him to open to me. If I had not, my stage would have become his war zone.

We both came to an understanding of our different perspectives and our similar desires. He gave me a wonderful opportunity to demonstrate the power of emotional intelligence.

> The question is not, "How can I get them to see?" but instead, "How do I want them to feel?" Everyone should leave the table feeling heard and respected, regardless of the outcome.

If you force people to see your way, they may *see* briefly, then go away looking for reasons to make you wrong. They *see* while thinking you are a *jerk* or an *idiot* regardless of how smart you are. No one likes to feel wrong or stupid.

Respect is built on force only in times of crisis. At all other times, it is built on a genuine demonstration of how much you honor those you are speaking to as intelligent beings, even if you disagree with them. You suspend your impulse to defend so you can engage the humans you are with.

> Would you rather win as a jerk or find the win-win as a sage? Focus on connecting instead of proving and you're more likely to find ways to influence.

To make a solid connection with others, you must be *willing* to listen to ideas contrary to yours, have the *desire* to create an outcome that works for everyone, and muster the *courage* to jump into the unknown where you might take on new opinions and ideas. You need to be open to the possibility that the conversation could change your mind as well.

The quicker you act on creating an open relationship, the better off you'll be when you face more difficult conflicts down the road. As soon as you meet people, if you want a good working relationship with them, you should arrange for a meeting to discuss how you hope to work together BEFORE any damage is done. Then, when you are emotionally affected by a conversation or situation, address it as soon as possible.

Even if you agreed on how you will work together, your emotions will still be triggered when you interact with the person or team. If you feel overwhelmed by expectations and can't be present, you should let them know about your mental state BEFORE you pretend to listen. If you are hurt by someone's behavior, tell them how you feel and ask their intentions BEFORE you launch a counterattack. Be aware of your own fears of being rejected, looking wrong, or feeling stupid. Then, ask yourself if your fears are valid. If you aren't sure, be willing to give the person the benefit of the doubt BEFORE you assume the worst.

Willingness, desire, and courage leads to creativity—the ability to rise above your reactive brain to see options. When you notice your reactions and clear your mind and body, you are free to see what is at the source of an emotional reaction in others. Here are some common behaviors seen at work:

- **A need for approval or acceptance** can cause a person to refuse to take risks or take too many risks. It also shows up with people who stick to doing what is comfortable so they don't disappoint, or they never say no to anyone, promising too much. Generally, their actions are designed to either ward off criticism or to attract positive attention. It may take only a little acknowledgment, trust, and guidance to help people feel safe enough to take risks or say no when they need to.

- **A need to feel important, appreciated, and held in esteem** can drive people to overwork and to demand perfection from others. They may be hypersensitive to criticism and feedback. Instead of relying on their own expertise, they judge their performance against others, looking to stay one step above others so they don't feel inadequate. They may show up as arrogant as opposed to confident. You might find it difficult to compliment these people, especially if they won't acknowledge your abilities or they strive to keep you in place by reminding you of your faults. Keep your distance and maintain your strength by noticing their needs for attention and acknowledgment. Don't react. Tell them what they do well without comparing them to others. If you want them to act differently, look for the payoff for them to change—what goal do they want that your suggestions will help them achieve? Tying your ideas to their goals could activate both their willingness and desire to change. They need to see the payoff to heed your advice.

- **A need for prosperity, recognition, or safety** might lead a person to focus on amassing money, possessions, or promotions above all else. The difficulty with this mind-set is that there is no conception of when enough is enough. It is also a self-centered focus that ignores the needs and values of others. Whenever possible, publicly honor and reward people who have a sense of community to create a culture that values relationship over personal ambitions. Define success as a team function. Declare expectations that people will act with trust, respect, and support. Be sure you consciously model the behaviors you want others to demonstrate.

- **The need for achievement** drives the desire for quick results, which drives the slower, more accurate workers crazy. You want to work with both types of people—achievers and people who want to make sure the work is done correctly. Break work into smaller tasks so your achievers feel a sense of accomplishment sooner without losing too many details along the way.

- **The need to control, to be right, and to win** drive people to do what they can to avoid being judged as vulnerable, weak, stupid, worthless, or incompetent. The thought of letting anyone see their all-too-human flaws is unbearable. Your best defense is to gracefully and honestly mention to the person the need you think is causing the person's reactions, then make a direct request. For example, if you say, "I can tell you would like to control this project. I know you've had success in the past leading similar projects and teams, but I want to make sure everyone has a voice here since there is so much uncertainty around resources and outcomes. Would you be willing to support the team by letting everyone have a chance to speak in meetings, and actively allow views that oppose yours to be considered?" Or, if someone has a need to be right and they correct you in front of others, you might say, "I apologize for the oversight. I know accuracy is very important to you. In the future, could we discuss situations like this privately after the meeting instead of in public?" Don't be afraid to set boundaries. The loss of ideas and respect from the team is a far greater cost than the consequence of someone not liking what you ask them to do.

- **The need for harmony** keeps people from standing up for themselves when they are right or when they should take charge of a situation. Wounds fester and problems multiply as they try to smooth things over. To get the best results, show that it is safe for people to speak up, share ideas, and even make mistakes. Help these people to speak up by acknowledging the value of their unique ideas. Show that you trust them to lead and will be there to talk things through when they are unsure of what to do.

- **The need for consistency** can be seen in those who complain about change, no matter how inevitable or beneficial the outcomes may be. Help these people walk through all the scenarios around what could happen, and the possible consequences of the changes so they know what to expect. Then allow them time to adjust. Or, you can ask the complainer, "What is your request?" This helps them think about what they would like to see take place instead of obsessing on what horrible things could happen. If the request is unreasonable, acknowledge the answer, and then say, "Okay, what else could you ask for?" Eventually, they will get the point.

Need-based behaviors can be damaging, but they can have a positive effect as well, helping achieve desired results. For example, taking control is useful when there is a need to jump-start a stalled project. Practicing consistency keeps daily tasks on track. Remember, people's greatest needs are also their greatest strengths.

The key is to act from choice, not anger or disappointment. Identify when someone's actions are beneficial or detrimental to the people and task at hand. If you know the behavior isn't appropriate for the situation, then ask for what you would like to see instead.

It's also helpful to model the behavior you want. In other words, if you catch yourself reacting inappropriately to a situation based on your own need to control, be right, be heard, or stay safe, admit your need got the best of you, then change your behavior. Modeling self-awareness, vulnerability, and flexibility are signs of effective leadership no matter what position you hold.

Notice when you are pushing your opinion even though another point of view is valid, and then admit you were pushing when you should have been listening. Notice when you shut down because you don't want someone to speak, and then either seek the value in what the person is offering or ask to delay their comments until later when they can be addressed more fully (but don't forget to get back to the person).

Remember that each person has their own needs. Acknowledging their needs can strengthen the relationship and move the conversation forward. For example, I was complaining about my rigid, insensitive boss to a friend of mine. When I paused, she said she heard my frustration but that I should remember that my boss was "doing the best he could with what he had."

This made sense to me.

Then she said, "However, the depth of your life experiences and your knowledge of people are so much greater than his, it is your responsibility to model what patience, flexibility, and compassion look like."

Reluctantly, I took on the challenge.

She was right. With patience, I didn't react so quickly to my boss. I listened before offering my point of view. I began noticing when he did things well, especially the times he supported the growth of others. He began to soften up, saying "yes" to my ideas more often than "no." Over time, our relationship improved.

Also, remember to keep up your self-care regimen. Your capacity to resolve conflicts and work well with others is hindered by sleep deprivation, poor nutrition, noise pollution, personal problems, a lack of money, and a shortage of friends. Your mental house must be clean before you entertain guests.

The Emperor's New Clothes

Remember the children's story about the emperor's new clothes? The emperor was told his invisible clothing were the most magnificent robes on the planet. He couldn't see the clothes, but agreed with their assessment, not wanting to look stupid. Although he did look stupid parading around naked, no one would tell the emperor for fear of being killed.

If you pretend that your own emotions don't exist, you are as blind as the emperor. At any given moment, people can sense your emotions and, at the same time, you are sensing the emotional states of the people around you.

No matter how good you might think you are at hiding your emotions, they affect your communications and ability to connect. In fact, when you try to hide your emotions, you create the experience of talking to a blank wall, which creates anger, frustration, or fear in others. People can't read you so they don't feel safe speaking up, or they become agitated for no apparent reason. At the same time, they are picking up signals from the energy of the emotions you are hiding, which increases their discomfort. Poker faces confuse more than calm others.

Ignoring emotional clues in a person or in the environment is ignoring vital information. Have you ever walked into a room and felt the air was thick with conflict? You probably felt an urge to be somewhere else unless engaging in conflict is your pleasure. Even if you don't want to talk about the emotional energy you detect, why neglect the data you are receiving? Better to talk about what you sense and discuss the effect on the situation at hand. If you do, you might prompt an exploratory conversation that allows people to share how they feel and why. Then you can discuss what it would take to shift the emotional state to a more productive atmosphere.

Yes, there are times when talking about how you feel and what you need could be a bad choice. You might need to find the appropriate time. If you aren't sure, ask for permission to talk about the emotions you are sensing in the room. You might be shut down, or told when the time is more appropriate, but at least you brought up the topic and asked for something you felt was important.

You might ask to add *check-ins* to meeting agendas half-way through or at the end of the meetings so it becomes normal for people to express how they feel about what is going on. Check in on how people feel about the process as well as the interactions. If you make these conversations a part of the agenda, people feel more comfortable sharing their views.

Muster your courage to be the person who notices the elephant in the room. Although some people might call you a troublemaker, you are demonstrating the courageous leadership needed for people and teams to grow together.

The brain's purpose is to protect, but humans also crave connection. This means that desires, fears, doubts, and needs will compete, making collaboration difficult. You will always feel and encounter defensiveness, fighting, and hiding. Reactions to even minor remarks result in suppressed hostility, impatience, and frustration. For people to trust you and others to work well together, they must feel safe enough to talk about their feelings and needs, which is necessary for relieving stress and moving forward.

As humans, logical people act illogically together. Help others find humor, gratitude, and meaning in volatile, uncertain times to ensure the best ideas come forward.

Remember to relax your body, detach from your rambling thoughts, center yourself in the present moment, and then focus on how you want to feel and how you want your stories to end. Then laugh at yourself as often as you can. Humor will attract more people to listen to you than to your rational arguments. Yet remember that no matter what you do, sometimes you won't get all you had hoped for when working with others, but isn't it worth the attempt? At the end of the day, you can say you did what you could and feel good about it.

Approach People with a Beginner's Mind

There is one more technique I want to share to help you establish and maintain meaningful and healthy relationships. I do my best to practice the following technique whenever I'm resisting a process or person. Like all life lessons, I learned the power of this technique the hard way, when I realized how self-centered I was acting. I realized that using a *Beginner's Mind* is both a way to experience life and a tool for building strong relationships.

Practicing Beginner's Mind means you attempt to shift your mind-set to perceive things, situations, and people as if you had never seen them before. What might you notice or realize if this were the first time you were seeing a person or situation? You will observe details you ignored, discover meaning you hadn't considered, and encounter amazing things you would not have seen while wearing your blinder of *already knowing*.

The habit of *already knowing* doesn't just block your perception. When you live *already knowing*, you spend a lot of time feeling angry or bored. *Already knowing* stops you from listening, and failing to listen is one of the greatest turn-offs in any conversation. You will never find solutions for communication problems, marital difficulties, and faltering friendships if you already know the reasons for the problems and haven't found a solution that works for all.

> If you already know the answer to a problem you are facing, if you already know what someone is trying to say before they say it, if you already know the source of someone's problematic behavior before they have a chance to explain, and if you already know what is going to happen next in any situation, you leave no room for anything new to emerge.

Shunryu Suzuki, author of *Zen Mind, Beginners Mind*, said, "In the Beginners Mind there are many possibilities. In the expert, there are few."[2] Experts hold on to already knowing all the answers. You need fresh eyes and an open mind to see beyond your limits.

Instead, try to come from a place of *not knowing the answer*. To do this, quit trying to figure out what people are going to say before they stop talking. Quit conjuring quick opinions about ideas. Quit choosing to only be with people who think like you and be open to alternative points of view.

I first learned of Beginner's Mind while teaching classes in Taiwan and Thailand for the manufacturing plants that were a part of the U.S. company I was working for. However, I couldn't put Beginner's Mind to the test until I returned home where I was used to seeing the same things day in and day out. Once I was home, I forgot to try.

After a few years, Gloria, my Chinese colleague who had never been out of Taiwan, came to the U.S. to learn to teach a class. It was mid-December, when Phoenix, Arizona, is filled with both human and avian winter visitors. I always noticed the crowds. Nothing seemed crowded to her. That was the first moment I realized how different she saw the city I was born in and rarely noticed as I drove to and from work every day.

I enjoyed showing her around, watching her delight in things I took for granted, like the big new buildings, huge parking lots, and cowboy-themed restaurants.

The biggest surprise happened when I took her to visit my home. I lived on a golf course. The lakes were always filled with ducks that time of year. As we neared my home, she saw the hundreds of ducks and said, "Oh, in Taiwan, that would be free duck."

Just as I realized she saw the ducks as dinner, we passed a yield sign suggesting drivers stop for ducks crossing the road. I pointed at the sign and explained to her that most of us in Phoenix saw the migrating ducks as a joy or a nuisance, but never as food. We laughed at our different notion of the value of ducks.

On Friday, I was driving her from work to her hotel. It was already dark outside. I was tired, hungry, and angry with the winter visitors who chose to drive at rush hour when I wanted to quickly get home.

As we inched through traffic, Gloria started to scream. I was surprised to find she was excited, not scared. She pointed out the window. All I could see were houses.

When she saw the confusion on my face, she said, "The lights!" Then it hit me—she was pointing at Christmas lights! Although many Christmas lights are made in Taiwan, people don't hang them on houses there. You might find them on stores, but not on homes, and especially not the large displays we have in U.S. neighborhoods.

I made a U-turn and headed for a street where all the houses on the block put up thousands of lights and animated figures. Gloria jumped out of the car with her camera. As she took photographs to show off back home, I tried to view the scene through her eyes. It took a few minutes, but when I finally cleared my mind, the bright, flashing lights and beautiful colors shined more brightly than they had in years. I can't say it was like seeing Christmas lights for the first time, but I felt like a child experiencing the awesome state of "wow."

The experience was so heartwarming and pleasant, I committed to practice seeing with a Beginner's Mind for the next few days. With fresh eyes, I savored the graceful flight of a bird, the gentle droop of a flower, and the erratic jump of a grasshopper. Mastering the skill was easy if I took my time, enjoyed the moment, and chose to ponder things I liked.

However, while observing people, places, and events *I did not like*, the practice proved difficult. Impatience, judgment, and doubt clouded my view. Catching my reactions in the moment and releasing them so my brain was a blank slate took more than mindfulness. I needed to practice humility or I would fall back into rationalizing my perspective. This was the lesson I had to learn.

I was given the opportunity to practice with my cousin Stuart. Stuart grew up in Cleveland, Ohio, far from my home in Phoenix. Although he was always nice to me, his whiny, slow-paced voice irritated me so much I ended our rare phone conversations as soon as I could.

Stuart grew up, went to college, and then took a job in the factory of a large electronic components manufacturing company. When we were both in our late thirties, Stuart was transferred to a factory in Douglas, Arizona, just across the border from Mexico. He called to tell me of the move and his promotion to plant manager. I congratulated him and said I'd visit someday. The drive from Phoenix to Douglas is over four hours; I always found excuses to avoid making the trip. Consequently, I never visited him, missing his marriage to a woman he met in Mexico and the births of his three children.

One day, Stuart called to say, "Marcia, I've been transferred to a plant outside of Phoenix. My family can't come for three months. Let's meet for dinner."

The following Tuesday evening, I sat in a Chinese restaurant across the table from my cousin Stuart. I thought, "Here is my chance to practice Beginner's Mind." I vowed to listen to Stuart as if I had never heard him before. I also decided to uncover something amazing about Stuart; hasn't everyone accomplished something important or memorable? I vowed to find a gem in Stuart.

He talked. I listened. He droned on. My mission grew more tedious as the minutes passed. Finally, our waitress showed up and saved the day.

I pointed at my menu, but before I could order, Stuart looked up and spoke to her in Chinese. At first I was impressed, but after seeing the look of confusion on the waitress's face, I felt embarrassed.

Then Stuart said, "Oh, you don't speak Mandarin. You must speak Cantonese."

He then spoke to her in Cantonese. This time, she smiled and replied.

Amazed, I said, "Stuart, I know you speak Spanish. And from my travels in Asia, I've learned Mandarin and Cantonese are very different languages. You must have studied quite a few languages in college."

"Oh no," he replied, "not in college. I run factories. People come from all over. I just listen and I pick it up."

I found something amazing about Stuart.

At that point, his whine transformed into a sing-songy cadence. Stuart turned into a fascinating person. I was eager to hear his stories. It was pleasant listening to cousin Stuart after all.

How many people have you blocked out of your life by erecting a wall of judgments and opinions? How many friends, coworkers, and closer or distant relatives do you react to because of behavior they displayed months, if not years, ago? What activities do you avoid because of your unpleasant memories? What parts of your work do you dodge based on past disappointments? We are so quick to judge and refuse to see what else is possible. There is so much more to any person, place, and event than your mind habitually allows you to see.

When observing a person, place, or event, you have two choices—clear your mind and see with fresh eyes or frame the view in past experiences. If you look through a filter of memories, old judgments, and stale opinions, you'll be stuck in the past. You'll only see what you expect. If you instead observe with a Beginner's Mind, you open yourself to surprise.

I was lucky to learn this lesson. A year after our dinner, Stuart was in Mexico sleeping by himself in a house warmed by a space heater. During the night, a drape near the heater caught fire. Stuart, a heavy sleeper, died in his sleep in the burning house.

At his funeral, I recognized his wife and children only because he showed me their photographs at dinner. Regretfully, I never found the time to drive to Douglas to meet them.

After the funeral service, I followed the crowd to his home. As is practice in our religion, we gathered to eat and share stories about the deceased to celebrate his or her life. Everyone was taking turns telling their stories about Stuart. When it was my turn, I recounted the anecdote about our night at the Chinese restaurant. They all laughed and thanked me for characterizing Stuart's many layers so well.

Before I could sit down, his mother said, "Let me tell you some other fabulous things about Stuart. Did you know he loved music? He wrote nearly a hundred folk songs. He wrote three symphonies! All this, and he never took a music lesson in his life. He also loved poetry. He wrote lyrics for many of his songs. And did you know he changed his religion? I wasn't happy about that, until I had the chance to spend a weekend with him visiting small-town congregations around Arizona. My anger melted as I watched him teach his philosophy of love to the children."

I promised my aunt that every opportunity I had, I would share my story about Stuart with others. It's not only a great lesson, it's my way of honoring a great man I barely knew.

There's nothing more life-affirming than death. When we are faced with mortality, people matter. Little things count. We see clouds crawl across the sky and hear whispers of angels in the trees. Unfortunately, this window to the beautiful intricacies of life stays open only for a few days. It slowly closes as we get busy again with our normal routines.

Don't let illness, loss, and death be your only fleeting reminders of the magnificence of life. Practice Beginner's Mind. Experience the pleasures of this planet. Savor the beauty in every soul you meet.

Be curious. Enter every conversation wanting to learn more than you already know. Seek to see a broader picture than the one you carry in your mind. You will see new ways to deal with challenges. Plus, people will find you much more interesting.

Cultivating the habit of seeing with a Beginner's Mind will open your heart as well as your mind. Not only will people seem more tolerable, even humorous, your entire spirit will be enlarged by the generous, life-giving quality of love.

■ *Practical Tips*

1. Before your next conversation or meeting, practice the Presence Routine of RELAX—DETACH—CENTER—FOCUS to clear your mind and needs. Then when you notice negative reactions in people's faces, bodies, and words, consider what they need and value as you decide what to say and how to act.

2. When you find yourself leading or working with a team on a project and conflict is in the air, suggest having a conversation where people can express their feelings and needs. Put the unspoken on the table so everyone can view what emotions might be blocking progress. Then ask what is needed to move forward. Ask people not to judge what is shared so everyone feels safe to share their ideas.

3. Identify one person and one situation where you can practice using Beginner's Mind. Repeat this exercise at least three times a week.

"Leadership is not about what you know,
it is about what you are willing to learn."
—Sid Ridgley

CHAPTER 6
INSPIRING GREATNESS

The Power of "I Want To"

In my last corporate job, I was hired as the corporate training manager for a semiconductor corporation, responsible for the *people side* of business. The company was in financial trouble but the leaders had a plan. They wanted to change everything, including the products, the markets, and the organizational structure. I was tasked with supporting the effort by helping develop both leaders and teams. I created customized courses in leadership development, personal effectiveness, and team success. After nine months, the shift was taking place successfully. Not only were we going to survive, we were on our way to success.

I was eager to explore ways to build on our success. I set up a meeting to share ideas with my boss. When we met, I pulled out my list. He waved me off saying, "I already have a plan for you. You are doing such a good job, the CEO and I decided you should also manage the factory training and trainers."

I balked. It seemed a distraction from my work in progress and I had no clue what went on in the factory. It was skill-based training outside of my expertise and interest. I also knew the three factory trainers had been managed by two other departments in the last sixteen months. They had been moved into manufacturing, then to process engineering, and now, they were being placed under human resources. This had to be a drain on their morale.

My boss answered my concerns by saying, "Don't worry. It's a no-brainer. It's just three women who come to work, do their jobs, and then go home."

The hair on my back bristled. When was managing anyone a *no-brainer,* especially mediocre employees? He indicated it wasn't my choice, so I reluctantly accepted the responsibility. I resigned to at least provide the three trainers with a more permanent home.

I reviewed the techniques I taught in my management classes, and then scheduled an appointment with each one. Three days later, the first trainer came into my office. As she sat, I asked, "So, tell me, what's your vision?"

She looked confused.

I explained, "You know, what do you want for yourself in your job? Is there anything you'd like to learn? Is there something you'd like to do more or less of on the job?"

She thought about my questions before saying, "There is a new computer system on the floor. I'd like to create some new reporting forms. What we have is so outdated. It would help a lot if we had a better way to track people and what they're doing."

"Great," I said. "What's it going to take? How can I help you?"

"There's a class I can take. I can sign up if you approve the overtime."

We called for the class schedule. Together, we found a way to balance her work with the computer classes.

The second trainer came into my office. Again, I asked, "So, tell me, what's your vision?"

She looked confused.

I explained, "What do you want for yourself? How would you like to develop and grow?"

She thought about the question, shifted her body a few times, and then sheepishly said, "I'd like to be a supervisor."

"Great," I said. "What's it going to take? How can I help you?"

"I'm not sure."

"Can you ask some of the supervisors on the floor what they think? What did they do to earn their positions, and what did they wish they had learned before becoming a supervisor? Once you interview them, you can create a list of things to learn and do that will prepare you to supervise."

"Sure, I can do that"

"Good. Find out, then we can work out a plan together." She came back a week later with her list of things she wanted to learn. We created a development plan. I also helped her find one of the factory supervisors to mentor her as she worked through her plan.

The third trainer came into my office. So as not to confuse her, I skipped the vision question and asked, "How would you like to develop yourself and how can I help you?"

She sighed and shut her eyes. Tears began to roll down her cheeks. Finally, she said, "I've worked here for sixteen years. This is the first time anyone asked me that."

After these meetings, do you think these trainers acted as my boss had described them, as people who came to work, did their jobs, and then left?

Hardly. My greatest problem was managing their overtime. The first trainer was rewarded for her new reporting system. The second trainer became the company's first factory training supervisor a year later after a super successful IPO had us scrambling to hire new trainers. The third trainer continued to be consistent, reliable, and helpful to everyone she met. The high evaluations they received from those they trained reflected their renewed motivation to work.

The point of the story is not to tout my accomplishment. Success should be given to the management programs I had been teaching over the years. I was practicing what I taught. The lesson I learned is that the difference in their productivity had nothing to do with their knowledge and skills. The results depended on their emotional commitment. Their performance was based on *how they felt* while doing the job, not on how well they knew how to do it.

> It's a simple formula. If *I want to* do a good job, I do it. If I don't feel like doing a good job, I don't, at least not to my maximum potential. My effort rests on *how I feel* in any given moment.

Even high achievers lose the drive to work at their best if their leaders don't seek to understand and help them meet their needs, especially the needs for accomplishment, recognition, autonomy, and a contribution that feels meaningful. The environment can also hinder productivity if people don't feel safe and respected. Cultures full of fear, mistrust, and cynicism poison motivation.

People do good work when they *want to* do it. Willingness is not enough. They must have a personal payoff, which could include making a difference for others, before they will fully engage with their tasks. This desire not only frees them to do good work, aspiring to achieve also causes a chemical reaction that increases the efficiency of brain activity and thus, performance.

In short, no matter how strong your work ethic is, when factors in your environment detract from *how good you feel* when you're working, the result is a decrease in the energy available to perform. Other factors such as *anger, anxiety,* and *determination* may motivate you for a while, but sooner or later you must feel *pride* in your work, that you are *valued* by your leaders and *acknowledged* by your peers, and have some *fun* in the process to maintain the motivation to work at your peak.

> The culture of a team or organization
> is defined by the overriding emotional state.

If you look at a team or an organization as an organism, you will find the dominant emotions felt by the people determine the quality of the output. Just as you have an Optimal Productive State based on your emotions, so do groups. Teams are energetic or frustrated, inspired or dejected, connected or chaotic, optimistic or dispirited, and aligned or contentious. The ability of the team to make decisions and to deliver a star performance is determined by how the people *feel* about the task, about each other, and about the leadership they report to.

When people feel afraid, angry, frustrated, stressed, or depressed, their work suffers. They cannot efficiently process information. They don't feel like being creative. Their emotions distort or disable logical thought. When this happens in a team setting, dysfunction multiplies.

Just as individuals can burn out, organizations can burn out, too. Chronically heavy workloads, no time for personal development, lack of group and individual recognition, and a preference to put off or ignore anything related to emotions drains the energy out of the organization. Symptoms include a high rate of turnover, an increase in absenteeism, low morale, reduced productivity, passive resistance to improve, increased conflict, and hopeless attitudes.

Emotions are contagious. Anger or fear can quickly spread. Even if you are doing something else, if you are near a fearful or angry person, your brain will pick up the cues and respond. Either your brain will try to protect you, causing distress, or you will mirror the dominant emotion in the room. An organization is a collective brain. Each person is a potential trigger.

Positive emotions can spread as well. Just as your brain works most efficiently when you feel positive emotions, so does an organization or team.

The highest priority for the leader should be
to influence the emotional state of the team.

If you are tasked with the growth of a team or business, then you must inspire a culture of positive emotions. You need to constantly take the pulse of the emotions of the team and determine how to keep it upbeat and hopeful, even in a downbeat economy. In the worst of times, people still need to feel they can rely on each other.

The research now overwhelmingly proves that managers who don't care about how people feel, who just want to get the job done, and who pressure people and use fear as a motivator are less effective than their concerned counterparts. The managers who instead learn about the values, priorities, and needs of the individuals, and then align this information with the business goals to create a vision that inspires positive emotional reactions, create a culture where people choose to work at their best.

Intimate Allies

Leadership is about relationships. This may sound contrary to the old rule, "Don't get too close to your employees." Craig Taylor, senior VP for TalentKeepers, a leading U.S. retention firm, said, "The evidence points in one direction: Employees want a leader who knows them, understands them, treats them fairly, and is someone whom they can trust."

In other words, as Paul Pearsall wrote in *The Heart's Code*, managers need to become intimate allies with their employees.[1]

When they come to know what each person wants, needs, fears and doubts, leaders can then determine how each employee can enjoy their work and feel worthwhile.

Gone is the mantra, "I treat everyone the same." Today, leaders must recognize people as individuals.

When people love coming to work, when they define their workplaces as pleasant, even fun, and they enjoy the frequent opportunities to talk with their supervisors and leaders, then the positive culture will drive great results. This will be the new definition of a "well-oiled machine."

Who's Driving the Bus

The results of motivation differs from inspiration. Whereas motivation drives action, inspiration arouses emotion. Over time, uninspired employees run out of gas. They burn out, become angry, and often their health declines.

> An optimally productive culture
> must be fueled by inspiration.

Many corporations seek to hire the "right" people" and to let go of the bottom 20 percent who don't measure up. The goal is to put the right butts on the right seats in the bus. The focus is on talent, where the person with the right intelligence and skills is right for the job.

Yet what happens when the bus is on the open road? Will the riders volunteer to help steer, eagerly seeking shortcuts and ways to maneuver around roadblocks? What happens when the bus breaks down? Will the riders jump out of their seats to fix it? Will they jump to help their fellow passengers? If the weather gets bad, the road grows narrow, and newer busses zoom by, will the riders stay in their seats or will they seek a better ride in a different bus as soon as the weather clears up?

Now more than ever, leaders need to stay on track with developing their emotional intelligence to discover ways of increasing rapport and commitment at work. Talent will always be important but it won't be the deciding factor in the next generation of successful companies. Long-term success will be based on a culture of passion, dedication, and sense of purpose rallied by the leaders.

Patrick Harker, president of the Federal Reserve Bank of Philadelphia and former dean of the Wharton School, compared business culture to physics. "It's all about vibrations and the frequencies we create. We see that all the time in business—the harmonics of an organization. We tend to have this very mechanistic, Newtonian view of companies, but the reality is that leaders impose a kind of frequency on a company."

What we need are leaders who act as symphony conductors, not bus drivers.

Why Leaders Avoid Their #1 Responsibility

"The most important need for leaders today..." my ears perked up. The speaker, a well-known tech leader, was addressing an audience of HR professionals. He had presented some facts showing the abysmal state of employee engagement, numbers I have sadly, been sharing for years. I was hoping for a brilliant insight when he said leaders most needed, "...to hold meaningful one-on-one conversations with their employees." Wasn't this the message I was asked to deliver over thirty years ago, when I taught my first management training class? Leaders avoid the best way to improve engagement.

Most people prioritize what they are good at, leaving the difficult tasks at the bottom of the list. So, it makes sense that leaders avoid one-on-one conversations because humans are unpredictable and messy. They are emotional by nature and few leaders want to deal with other people's emotions. They don't want to feel the emotions themselves, and they don't know what to do when emotions arise. Because there is no guarantee how any conversation will turn out, leaders avoid what could turn out badly.

As you learned earlier, emotions are normal. We are feeling emotions throughout the day. They aren't bad; they simply reflect energy moving through the body. Acknowledging emotions in a conversation can lead to discovering important information needed to break through blocks, make good decisions, and take a positive step forward.

Even if people trust you to be honest with them, they need to know it's okay to be themselves no matter what they are experiencing, without worrying about being negatively judged.

> What leaders avoid—emotional expression—
> is their best chance to connect.

Most leaders rationalize their avoidance by saying things like, "If I encourage people to talk about their feelings, I will say things I wouldn't normally say." Or, "I don't have time for their dramas." The business world is full of aphorisms that declare, "Only the tough survive." It makes sense that no one wants to be the leader that breaks the rules and allows people to feel. The entire organization becomes one big receptacle of stuffed emotions.

You Can't Fix All the Problems

I have found that leaders avoid conversations where emotions might be present for two reasons:

1. When someone expresses an emotion, most leaders feel an emotion in response, making them uncomfortable with their own feelings as well as the ones the person is expressing.

2. The leader then feels the need to make the person feel better or to solve the problem that is causing the anger, fear, or frustration the person is experiencing. The problem is, the leader can't fix the person or easily resolve the situation. The leader feels inadequate and then worries about being judged as a bad leader.

The irony is that if you try to fix the person, you make them feel wrong or weak for expressing how they feel. Or, if you try to fix the situation, you might make promises you can't keep.

The best you can do is to notice how you feel, clear your mind, center your awareness, and then choose to feel calm, compassionate, and curious. Allowing people to fully express themselves without judgment will help you both explore the situation more fully and then together, find the best way to move forward.

If you stay calm, they will calm down, too. Then you can ask questions to help them determine what they think they are not getting in the situation that is triggering their emotions. Understanding how emotions factor into the situation makes you wise. Creating a safe space to talk about emotions makes you strong. Leaders who have the courage to stay present and allow for emotional expression can have meaningful conversations that increase engagement, innovation, and results.

Appreciating instead of avoiding
someone's experience opens the
door to finding real solutions.

I know this is easier said than done. Staying present when people are emotional while noticing and releasing your own feelings can be scary and even painful. Here are six tips for what to do when emotions arise during difficult conversations:

1. **Take a breath,** release your tension, and be quiet. Give people a moment to recoup so they don't feel badly for reacting.
2. **Allow the reaction to happen.** They might apologize or ask to leave. Tell them you understand why they are reacting so they feel normal instead of defective.
3. **Don't try to quickly fix the person or the problem.** If the person is smart and resourceful, it is better to give them a quiet moment to relax. Then you can

ask questions to learn more about how they see the situation and what they need to move forward. This will help them think more rationally.

4. **If they get defensive, don't fuel the fire.** Don't get angry in return or disengage. Whether they are mad at you or others, give them a moment to vent to release the steam. If the emotions don't subside, seek to set another meeting when the person can more comfortably look at solutions with you.

5. **If they are afraid, ask what consequences they fear** and then listen to their answer. Don't tell them they shouldn't feel afraid. Encourage them to speak by asking a few questions that show you are curious and you care. What are they afraid they will lose in the future? What else could happen? What can you do to support them through the change? Listen with curiosity, care, and compassion. You can help them discern assumptions from reality where they might see a possible way forward.

6. **Before you end the conversation, ask them to articulate what they discovered or learned.** Articulating insights helps people feel stronger. Identifying what they are learning gives them a sense of control.

Being an inspiring leader means you can sort things out together no matter what people feel. People are emotional. If you judge or avoid their reactions, you are judging or avoiding them as humans. That never feels good. See the person in front of you as doing his or her best with what he or she knows now. From this perspective, you might have an amazing conversation that could surprise both of you.

Remember, the extra effort that drives a company's competitive edge rests on how good people feel over time. Leaders must commit to listening to their people. If they make time to listen even when time is scarce, they will know how to lead people out of fear, anger, and resignation into the space of possibility.

The return on investment for listening, understanding, and caring is great. In addition to more profit and success, a new light will be shining in your workplace. The light will come from the eyes of the employees.

The Excuse of Time

When I teach coaching skills to leaders, I'm often asked how to make the time for having deep conversations when there is so much work to get done. Have you ever felt you had so much to do you didn't have time to spend with people? The emails, calls, and knocks on the door make you cringe. Spending time with people gets in the way of what feels to be most important.

The irony is that the focus on getting work done over being with people is the reason why many people leave their jobs, either mentally or physically. Forcing people to focus on the task guarantees errors, gaps, and less than stellar results. No wonder everyone feels stressed, frustrated, disappointed, and unfulfilled.

> Focusing on the processes, tasks, and milestones while ignoring the human needs can sabotage the best outcomes.

Your impatience is your greatest pitfall. People you work with become a means to the end instead of them being respected partners working to achieve something together. No one feels valued or important in this scenario, yet people need to feel valued and important to sustain their desire to give their best efforts.

To get good results, you must focus more on the people than on problems and tasks. Then trust they will give their best efforts to get the work done. Managers and team members must count on each other to achieve the vision of the results created together. You need to appreciate everyone's efforts and invite others to ask for help when they need it so nothing falls through the cracks. Seek to understand other people's needs and hopes whenever you engage in a conversation.

> Effective leadership requires you let spending time with people get in the way.

Taking time for meaningful conversations will try your patience. Recognizing when you discount people when you feel pressure to get work done is a great awareness to have. Feel impatient and make the time anyway.

No matter how long your to-do list is, don't hide from the people who want a piece of your precious time. When people get in the way of your work, they are giving you the wonderful opportunity to connect with them so they are inspired to achieve more. The conversations don't always turn out well but missing the chance have a memorable moment with an employee who asks to speak with you can harm relationships and results beyond the lost work you thought was more important.

Building a high-trust, high-performance environment requires you treat everyone as a significant human being. Values, strengths, and talents will differ as well as personalities. People will rub each other the wrong way as styles clash. However, the underlying respect for what each other contributes to the shared vision and the agree-on goals is the thread that keeps everything running well.

Stopping your work to take a moment out of your day to fully see the person in front of you is the greatest gift you can give to them. We all long to be seen, be understood, and feel valued for who we are beyond what we do. This is how you inspire the human heart to soar. It's amazing how much good work can then get done.

Reacting to Hurtful Behavior

When it comes to dealing with people you find most difficult—who react by complaining, blaming, competing, slapping down with arrogance, or sabotaging with complacency—instead of reacting to their behavior, you now know how to stay calm, curious, and confident in your response. This will at least decrease your stress. Then if you can find the willingness and goals that would encourage these people to explore different behaviors and perspectives with you, you might be able to change their minds. Or, you might find it is time to move them out so their behavior doesn't have a negative impact on your team's culture.

In fact, once you take charge of your emotional reactions and can stand more solidly in the present moment, the needs that are triggering their reactions will be transparent. No matter how insensitively a person may behave, few people on this planet focus their thoughts and actions on how they can hurt someone else for the pleasure of it. Rudeness, shaming, misunderstandings, and offensiveness often happen when people are grasping for attention, control, or appreciation, not because of the desire to hurt.

You often hear, "It's not my job." "That will never work here." "I don't have time to do that presentation." It is often *fear* at the root of these statements, not laziness, haughtiness, or apathy. Their reptilian brains are seeking protection. Even an act of vengeance has the fear of losing or the anger of loss at the source of the action.

It's true that some people put forth a challenge to see "what stuff you're made of." Yet, even in these cases, their actions aren't motivated by the desire to make you look stupid. They are either trying to help you step up or trying to eradicate their own feelings of inadequacy by proving they are better than you. If they are trying to help you reach for your higher potential, then they truly honor your talent. If they are using you to build themselves up, then recognize they must think you are worthy of being a benchmark.

Before you react, ask yourself the following questions:

- What is driving them to act that way?
- What is their brain protecting?
- Are they afraid of not being heard, of being made wrong, of not being acknowledged, or of failing?
- Do they feel I've disrespected them or devalued their ideas?
- Did they have an expectation that I failed to fulfill?
- Do I intimidate them and are they afraid I won't approve of or like them?
- Are they concerned that others won't find their ideas credible or worthy of respect?
- Have I created a safe space so they can speak their mind? Do I *want* them to feel safe enough to speak their mind?

You may be able to answer these questions on your own. You may have to ask the person. If you want to resolve a situation or coach a person through a problem, use the SET-C method of inquiry.

1. Ask them to tell the **STORY** from their point of view. Be curious. Don't assume you know anything.
2. Identify the **EMOTION(S)** they are feeling.
3. Look for the possible **TRIGGERS.** You might ask them to verify what you perceive are their emotions and triggers. If you are wrong, they will probably tell you what they believe is true for them, which

will deepen your conversation. Being wrong in your assessment is okay, and possibly helpful.

4. **CHOOSE** how you want to redirect the conversation. Ask them what they need to ask for to resolve the situation. If they admit they have no control over the source of their stress, ask what it would take for them to let go. Sometimes all you need to do is help people to understand what they are feeling—and why—and they will know for themselves what they need to do.

Remember, before you begin the conversation, determine if you can speak neutrally. How are you feeling? Can you talk to them in such a way that they would welcome the opportunity to discover possible options of how to be together? You may need to take a deep breath, stop your own mental chatter, center yourself in the present, and then focus on the outcome. To have an effective but difficult conversation, they must have a strong sense of *psychological safety* to honestly reflect on their own thoughts and openly interact with you.

Psychological Safety

I teach leadership for a global corporation where we start each day of training with a "Safety Moment." The exercise is designed to decrease physical accidents. When I try to teach these same leaders how to make people feel comfortable and safe in conversations, especially ones that might trigger emotions and prompt opinions contrary to their own, the leaders claim a lack of time and value. ***Leaders often don't connect the need for psychological safety to the need for physical safety.***

Harvard professor Dr. Amy Edmondson says, "Psychological safety describes the individuals' perceptions about the ***consequences of interpersonal risk*** in their work environment. It consists of taken-for-granted beliefs about how others will respond when one puts oneself on the line, such as by asking a question, seeking feedback, reporting a mistake, or proposing a new idea."[2]

The brain will filter what people say or stop them from speaking if there is any indication—real or not—that they will be embarrassed or hurt. This is an automatic response that happens before you can use logic to assess the situation. Most people just justify their silence or defensiveness.

I occasionally co-teach classes with colleagues. When I feel safe with my partner, the experience is joyful and participant evaluations are high. When instead, my partner gives me advice with little or no praise and steps in to "help" without asking, the evaluations are mediocre no matter how well I know the material and tell myself to accept that my colleague is just trying to help.

My experience is common. When you feel safe with someone, you feel freer to engage in creative conversations and trials. When you feel psychologically protected, you are more open to learn, more willing to help others out, and will report higher job satisfaction.

When you don't feel psychologically safe, the outcome of each step you take feels unpredictable and scary. The fear can be compared to what children of alcoholic parents feel. In addition to fear, the prolonged lack of safety can trigger pessimism and emotional numbness. Self-worth and confidence could plummet, resulting in low productivity and more stress-related illnesses, turnover, and accidents. ***Psychological safety affects physical safety.***

Ask yourself these questions:

- Do I feel I can express my thoughts without being judged?
- Do I believe I can talk about how I feel?
- Do I feel valued for who I am, not just the goals I cross off my list?

Then ask your employees to ask themselves these questions, too. Actively encourage people to ask questions, offer ideas, build on their mistakes, and comfortably disagree with you while staying open to being changed by what they offer.

But words aren't enough. You can't just tell people they should trust you or there is nothing to fear. They may have been judged, embarrassed, or retaliated against in the past.

> **Never assume trust; you need to consciously build it into every relationship.**

For people to feel you are sincerely open to them, let your ego fade into the background. Notice when a judgment creeps in, when you are formulating your answer instead of listening, and when your muscles tighten up with impatience or resistance. Practice these steps during the next conversation you have:

1. **Take clues from your body.** Use your emotional awareness to recognize when you are getting irritated, anxious to speak, or you have the urge to step in and fix the situation without permission.

2. **Choose how you want to feel.** If you want people to feel curious, calm, or hopeful, shift to feel this emotion yourself. Breathe and feel your chosen emotion before you enter the room. Use this as your anchor to reset your emotions during your conversations.

3. **Assess your level of respect.** If you don't respect them, they will not feel safe with you. What do you appreciate about the person or people you are with? Recall good acts or intentions to shift back to respect.

4. **Determine what people need from you.** Do they need to know it is okay to share ideas not fully fleshed out? Do they need you to encourage them to take risks? What can you say to demonstrate you understand why they feel uncomfortable, then ask what it would take for them to be willing to share their ideas or try something else.

The Roadway to Success

In their article, *Developing Emotionally Intelligent Organizations,* Richard Boyatzis and Ellen Van Oosten described the shift in thinking of the leaders at Roadway, a trucking company, and the measurable success after integrating emotional intelligence into their corporate culture.[3] They described how one manager faced losing one of Roadway's largest clients, Specialty Glassware, due to excessive breakage on the dock.

The manager reported that when he shifted the problem into a group challenge instead of owning responsibility, he could shift out of his fear and into possibility. He gathered his entire crew to meet with the top executives from Specialty Glassware. Instead of complaining, the client gave the dock workers a presentation about their company, including their vision, processes, and strategy, which included delivering their products using Roadway trucks. At the end of the program, the visiting executives presented each dock worker with a commemorative mug made by Specialty Glassware.

The problem of breakage soon disappeared. The crew felt included and significant. This led to finding ways to be more careful and to help Specialty Glassware succeed.

Overall, Roadway had shifted to a company where everyone—executives, managers, drivers, dock workers, and staff—talked with pride and excitement about what it meant to work at Roadway. Their excitement inspired confidence in their customers, increasing sales. They also saw a decrease in injuries and accidents by nearly one half than before the organizational changes. They attributed these success to the culture that encouraged and used emotional expression.

Their goals included:

- increasing self-awareness at all levels by teaching and rewarding emotional intelligence;
- positioning leaders to develop emerging leaders at every level;

- developing the capabilities to achieve breakthrough performance by identifying training needs and coaching people to implement the needed competencies; and
- broadening the employees' understanding of issues crucial for long-term economic performance.

The strategy centered on a nine-day training curriculum that spanned six months, covering emotional intelligence, business strategy, systems thinking, marketing, finance, and techniques in appreciative inquiry. The classes included simulations where managers could practice new habits of emotional self-awareness and choice in "real time." They also coached each other to discover their passions—what they truly wanted out of life and work. Then, using information from a 360-degree assessment of their emotional competencies, the leaders created a personal vision and plan for development. This activity helped fuel the desire for making changes to improve their leadership behavior.

In addition to follow-up coaching, the leaders were given external coaches to help them at each step in the process. The coaches provided reflection and reality-testing as the leaders went through the training and implementation back on the job. Roadway felt the coaching was crucial to the success of the program.

Back on the job, the leaders then shared much of what they learned with their teams, both individually and in groups. They formed problem-solving teams. New organizational norms formed across the company. Quality and sales soared. A mechanic and driver discovered a way to save the company $130,000 per year on one route, more than both their salaries combined.

Emotions are contagious. New leaders must acknowledge the human spirit. They must model the behavior they want to see in others, including living by their own values, speaking the truth with compassion, showing confidence, trusting others, exhibiting social responsibility, maintaining flexibility and tolerance, and having a sense of humor. They must know how to outsmart their own brains to make the right choices. These choices should reflect a growing buzz of excitement in the organization.

Can you accept this mantle of power? The challenge is to develop emotionally intelligent organizations that ring with the joyous noise of laughter while allowing full human beings to come to work. Leaders who orchestrate these cultures will have a competitive advantage for many years to come.

■ *Practical Tips*

1. Turn passion into performance by helping people discover and align their values with their work.
2. Create an emotionally intelligent culture by integrating the skills and concepts of EI into hiring, promotions. and recognition systems.
3. Encourage all employees to integrate the language of emotions into their work conversations. Provide training for employees and coaching for leaders to make the transition.
4. Expect leaders to model behavior that inspires trust, confidence, and caring among all employees.

5. Work with a coach to develop a personal vision and plan to increase your ability to outsmart your brain to make the best choices for yourself and to create a safe space for growth and innovation for others.

"We've never been here before; we can't know what will happen; we've got to have everybody's brains and voices in the game."
—Amy Edmondson

APPENDIX A
NAME THAT EMOTION

An Inventory of Feelings to Increase Your Emotional Discernment and Comprehension

"Emotions" refers to the mental and physiological states characterized as feelings. It's often hard to put a name on what you're experiencing. It's likely that your brain is processing more than one reaction at a time. Not only do feelings overlap and blend, but there are hundreds of emotions, each with many gradations of intensity, that make emotional awareness a difficult skill to master.

The more adept you are at discerning what you are feeling, the greater will be your ability to manage your behavior. You can choose to act in the moment based on possibilities instead of reacting in the moment based on habit. In other words, you respond with intelligence instead of impulse. The result is greater effectiveness, productivity and confidence. And, as you come to comprehend your own emotions and behavior, you increase your understanding for what drives the actions of those around you. Emotional intelligence is a key factor to enhancing your quality of life.

For the next two weeks, set your phone or watch to alarm four times a day. At the times listed on the schedule, or ones more convenient for you, fill in the blanks with **1) what you are feeling** and **2) what you think is causing you to feel this way**. Use the lists below and on the next two pages to help you identify what you are feeling. If you are with other people or sleeping during the times listed, adjust the hours on the assessment to fit your schedule. The exact times are not essential. However, it's important to assess what you are feeling *in the moment* instead of relying on memory.

Remember, you are seeking to understand your feelings, not trying to change them. They are not right or wrong. Therefore, honesty is critical. However, recognition alone can diffuse or increase an emotional reaction. You may find that over time, the intensity of some moods decreases, while other sensations, hopefully the more pleasant ones, increase. Use this list to help you identify the specific emotions if you can.

Anger

Fury	Hostile	Offended
Enraged	Rebellious	Distrustful
Hateful	Resistant	Cynical
Resentful	Envious	Wary
Exasperated	Superior	Cautious
Annoyed	Defiant	
Irritated	Disgusted	**Fear**
Vengeful	Repulsed	Apprehensive
Cheated	Appalled	Nervous

Panicky
Worried
Distressed
Edgy
Restless
Frightened
Threatened
Troubled
Overwhelmed
Wound-Up
Impatient
Testy

Disheartened
Baffled
Confused
Lost
Disoriented
Disconnected
Trapped
Lonely
Isolated
Sad
Miserable
Dejected
Gloomy
Desperate
Depressed
Devastated
Helpless
Weak
Exposed
Irritable

Serious
Somber
Disappointed
Hurt
Inadequate
Shy
Unloved
Abandoned
Frail
Out of sorts
Weary
Tired
Burned-Out
Unfeeling
Indifferent
Bored
Exhausted
Frustrated
Grumpy

Shame
Humiliated
Mortified
Embarrassed
Ashamed
Uncomfortable
Guilty
Regretful
Remorseful
Reflective
Sorrowful
Detached
Aloof

Surprise
Shocked
Startled
Stunned
Amazed
Astonished
Impressed

Impassioned
Enthusiastic
Excited
Aroused
Delirious
Passionate
Crazed
Euphoric
Thrilled
Competitive
Willful
Determined
Confident
Bold
Eager
Optimistic
Satisfied
Proud
Glowing

Happy
Joyful
Blissful
Amused
Delighted

Triumphant
Fortunate
Pleased
Silly
Dreamy
Enchanted
Appreciative
Grateful
Hopeful
Intrigued
Interested
Engrossed
Alive
Vivacious

Calm
Contented
Relieved

Peaceful
Relaxed
Fulfilled
Reserved
Comfortable
Receptive
Forgiving
Accepting
Loved
Serene

Regard
Adoring
Fond
Warm
Affectionate
Safe
Respectful

Friendly
Sympathetic
Generous
Loving
Compassionate

Other:
(Write Your Own)

Emotional Assessments

Week 1	Mon.	Tues.	Wed.	Thu.	Fri.	Sat.	Sun.
7:30 a.m.							
Feeling							
What's the source?							

Week 1	Mon.	Tues.	Wed.	Thu.	Fri.	Sat.	Sun.

11:00 a.m.

Feeling

What's the source?

3:00 p.m.

Feeling

What's the source?

9:00 p.m.

Feeling

What's the source?

Week 2	Mon.	Tues.	Wed.	Thu.	Fri.	Sat.	Sun.

7:30 a.m.

Feeling

What's the source?

11:00 a.m.

Feeling

What's the source?

3:00 p.m.

Feeling

What's the source?

Week 2	Mon.	Tues.	Wed.	Thu.	Fri.	Sat.	Sun.
9:00 p.m.							
Feeling							

What's the source?

What did you discover after tracking your emotions for two weeks?

What patterns did you find?

APPENDIX B
SELF-CARE CHECKLIST

Environment

- ☐ Is your office organized so you can find things easily?
- ☐ Are there more than two piles of papers, magazines, and books in your workspaces?
- ☐ Does your home provide you comfort and a peaceful place where you can think?
- ☐ Are your appliances in working order?
- ☐ Do you have back-up systems in case of electric failure, including a back-up energy source for your computers?
- ☐ Do you maintain your car regularly so everything works properly?
- ☐ Does your home have a smoke detector, fire extinguisher, and easy contact to the police?
- ☐ Do you keep enough home and office supplies so you don't run out?
- ☐ Do you find the colors and decor in your home and office pleasing?
- ☐ Is the temperature in your home and office comfortable?

Physical Health

- ☐ Do you sleep six to eight hours every day?
- ☐ Is your bed comfortable?
- ☐ Does your back feel fine after sitting in your chair at work?
- ☐ Do you eat fresh, healthful food almost every day?
- ☐ Do you exercise at least three times a week?
- ☐ Is your cholesterol count within the normal range?
- ☐ Do you drink at least five glasses of filtered water each day?
- ☐ Do you drink zero to two caffeinated drinks a day?
- ☐ Do you keep your sugar intake to a minimum?
- ☐ Do you get a medical physical annually?

Mental Health

- ☐ Do you wake up looking forward to your day?
- ☐ Do you take the time to acknowledge what you are grateful for each night?
- ☐ Do you take at least two vacations a year that refresh and energize you?
- ☐ Do you have someone in your life that hugs you regularly?
- ☐ Do you arrive at least five minutes early for your appointments?
- ☐ Do you take your time when driving?
- ☐ Do you promise only what you can deliver?
- ☐ Do you regularly explore new ways of perceiving the world?
- ☐ Do you have a good belly laugh at least once a day?
- ☐ Do you have at least two friends outside of your immediate family who you feel free to talk with about anything?

Money

- ☐ Do you have little or no debt?
- ☐ Do you save at least 10 percent of your income?
- ☐ Do you carry enough cash with you to cover emergencies?
- ☐ Are you compensated adequately for your work?
- ☐ Do you recover from financial disappointments quickly, knowing things will improve?
- ☐ Do you have savings to cover home, car, and health emergencies?
- ☐ Are you amply insured for your home, car, and health?
- ☐ Do you invest in your own career development so you can earn more in the future? Or, are you saving enough for your retirement?
- ☐ Do you have a special knowledge or skill that gives you job security?
- ☐ Do you have a reputable and knowledgeable financial advisor?

Relationships

- ☐ Do your family/friends/colleagues encourage your dreams?
- ☐ Do your family/friends/colleagues support your efforts to relieve your stress?
- ☐ Do you avoid no one?
- ☐ Have you said you were sorry to those who you've harmed in some way?
- ☐ Have you forgiven everyone who has hurt you?
- ☐ Do you tell those you love how much you care about them?

☐ Are you free of the need to fix other people?

☐ Are you free of people who repeatedly disappoint, frustrate, drain, or disrespect you?

☐ Do you feel significant with everyone you meet?

☐ Do you have a relationship with nature, your God, or a force outside of yourself that recharges your faith?

TOTAL BOXES CHECKED ON (date) _____

Tally up the boxes you checked.

Set goals to achieve the boxes left blank, one box at a time. Start with the category you scored the highest on so you begin on your strongest foot.

Work on this checklist until your score reaches at least 45. As your score increases, notice how much your energy increases as well.

FIND YOUR RESILIENCY RATE: HOW FAST DO YOU BOUNCE BACK?

Answer honestly; you have no one to fool but yourself.

1. Three unexpected expenses hit you in one month, making it difficult to pay your regular bills. Do you:
   A. Spend more, particularly on things that make you feel better.
   B. Review expenses to find any non-essentials to cut back on.
   C. Go into debt, figuring you'll make it up next month.
   D. Buy lottery tickets or make a risky investment that promises a quick turnaround on your money.

2. When a parent or friend criticizes you, do you:
   A. Avoid your parent or friend as much as possible.
   B. Revert to the way you reacted when you were 14 years old.
   C. Criticize back.
   D. Ask why the person is upset with you and try to understand what he or she is afraid of or needs from you to move forward.

3. When a friend disappoints you, do you:
    A. Talk about your feelings and explore what expectations you had, looking for the differences in your perceptions of what was said and what happened, and what you both need to renew the relationship.
    B. Let your friend know that you feel cheated and hurt, and you expect him or her to make due on the promise made to you.
    C. Leave, preferring friends who keep their word.
    D. Avoid your friend until you can get over your setback, giving your friend the benefit of the doubt.

4. When it becomes clear to you that a dream you had is going to take a lot more time, money, and/or energy than you thought, do you:
    A. Stop caring to protect yourself from further disappointment.
    B. Continue down the same path knowing you will win in the end.
    C. Take the time to feel your frustration before deciding what to do.
    D. Get real, finding a similar but easier goal to focus on, chalking up the loss to inexperience.

5. You had a bad day at work. Do you:
    A. Take it out on your family, your pet, or the other drivers on the road.
    B. Take it in stride as a part of your miserable life.
    C. Turn on the TV and watch until you're asleep.

    D. Find a way to shift your emotion so you can either think about your day more objectively or let it go and relax for the rest of the evening.

6. Your mate ends your relationship unexpectedly, do you:
   A. Quickly begin your search for the next one.
   B. Find ways to keep busy and avoid dating because you are not sure developing a new relationship is worth your time and energy.
   C. Look for ways to be where your former partner is, hoping he or she will want you back.
   D. Allow yourself time to explore what is at the source of any anger, embarrassment, or hurt you might be feeling so you can be clear on what you need to do to help you feel strong enough to seek a healthy relationship in the future.

7. Your flight is cancelled, leaving you to sit in the airport three hours, which forces you to miss a business meeting. Do you:
   A. Let the counter person know that the situation is unacceptable and that you will no longer be a customer on their airline.
   B. Go for a walk to release your anger. See if you can join the meeting by phone or computer.
   C. Beg to reschedule the meeting, blaming the airline.
   D. Go to the bar to drink until you can get on the next flight.

8. You found out you have a medical problem that will require extensive treatment and a lifestyle change. Do you:
   A. Seek support from others who have this disease, especially those who will let you express your anger and fears. Read

everything you can to understand what you are dealing with.

B. Deny the diagnosis, knowing you can heal yourself with herbs, healthy eating, and visualization.

C. Prepare for the worst to happen.

D. Isolate yourself, not letting anyone help you.

9. Your friend visits with his new dog. The dog breaks something of yours that didn't cost a lot, but had sentimental value. Do you:

A. Call your friend stupid for not controlling the dog.

B. Don't tell your friend, hiding the pieces so he or she won't feel badly. It was an accident. You should have dog-proofed the room.

C. Let your friend know it was an accident but that you are sad anyway. Sweep the pieces out of the way. When your friend leaves, say goodbye to the piece as you throw it away, remembering the person or experience it represented.

D. Quickly sweep up the pieces and throw them away so the incident doesn't ruin your visit.

10. The day after a party, you realize you did something you now regret and feel embarrassed about. Do you:

A. Beat yourself up, wondering how you could be so stupid.

B. Call everyone involved and apologize profusely.

C. Forgive yourself, look for the reason behind your behavior, and then determine what you need to do differently next time, if anything.

D. Vow to never hang out with those people again.

Resiliency Rate Scoring
Give yourself one point for the following answers:

1–B	2–D	3–A	4–C	5–D
6–D	7–B	8–A	9–C	10–C

If you scored at least 7, CONGRATULATIONS! You demonstrate a sound connection with your emotions. You are able to identify how you feel, acknowledge that your feelings represent a typical reaction, and then choose the best course of action in the moment to move on. Before you pat yourself on the back, answer these two questions:

a. Did you answer honestly or choose the items that were obviously correct? If you only circled the answers you thought you should, your intellect is firmly in control and hindering your growth.

b. Did you think the test was stupid? Scorning this little quiz could indicate you might not be ready to see what your emotions can tell you.

You're not alone if your intellect is in control. What's more important is recognizing if the quiz gave you any insights you want to remember and add to your goals. Being emotional intelligent requires you to engage in continual personal growth.

If you scored under 7, we applaud your honesty. Study your answers to see if you tend to fall back on one or more of the following destructive behaviors when things don't go your way:

1. **Blame others** for your disappointments without looking to see if your expectations of them may have been unrealistic

or out of your control. You feel they should do everything they can to make things right.

2. **Blame yourself** for being stupid, shortsighted, or inattentive.

3. **Ignore circumstances** and blaze forward, expecting things to work out in the end (they might, but calculating the odds and adjusting your goals might hedge your bets).

4. **React in harmful ways,** such as

   • displaying addictive behaviors (spending too much, lying or hiding the truth, and/or drinking or taking drugs to block out reality),

   • lashing out in anger,

   • avoiding confrontation,

   • giving up easily, or

   • numbing yourself with television, substances, or obsessive work.

5. **Ignore your emotions** since they only make you look and feel weak. Rarely let anyone know how you are feeling in the moment.

Coaching Tip: Practice the SET-C Technique.

   • STORY—Describe what you think is going on and why.

   • EMOTION—Identify what you are feeling.

   • TRIGGER—Look for what you are afraid of losing (i.e., respect, love, control) or what you feel you didn't get you thought you should have.

   • CHOOSE—Ask for what you need, or let go of what you can't control. Focus on how you want to feel and how you want the story to end. If letting go is difficult, hire a coach or therapist to help you make productive choices.

CHAPTER NOTES

CHAPTER 1: MASTERY—WHO'S IN CHARGE?

1 Michael Gazzaniga. *Who's in Charge: Free Will and the Science of the Brain.* Ecco, 2011, page 43.

2 Daniel Kahneman, *Thinking Fast and Slow,* Farrer, Straus & Giroux, 2011, page 32 begins the description of the brain's laziness, a reluctance to do more than what is strictly necessary.

3 David Bohm, *On Dialogue,* Routledge; 2nd Edition. 2004. The book is a collection of Bohm's essays and lectures exploring human communication, what stops us from connecting, and how we can transcend the barriers to create mutual understanding.

CHAPTER 2: DEVELOPING AWARENESS

1 Antonio Damasio, *Looking for Spinoza: Joy, Sorrow, and the Feeling Brain,* Harcourt Books, 2003, defines what a feeling is in Chapter 3. Feelings represent *how the body is being* as opposed to how you are labeling your reaction. Once you recognize the feeling in your body, you can label the sensation by assigning an emotion or two to the feeling, and then discern what is causing the emotion to arise.

2 Abraham Maslow (1943), "A Theory of Human Motivation." *Psychological Review,* 50 (4): 370–96. Maslow's hierarchy of needs is key to understanding human behavior, especially the need for love and belonging as more critical than fulfillment and personal growth. It is difficult to love yourself without the sense that others value you.

CHAPTER 3: **ACTIVATING CHOICE**

1 Joshua Freedman, Anabel L. Jensen., Marsha C. Rideout. *Handle with Care: The Emotional Intelligence Activity Book.* Six Seconds, 1998. 6Seconds.org was one of the first nonprofit organizations dedicated to the awareness of Emotional Intelligence and the need to teach it in schools to bring up emotionally intelligent children.

2 Robert M. Sapolsky, *Why Zebras Don't Get Ulcers: The updated guide to stress, stress-related diseases, and coping.* W. H. Freeman and Company, 1998. Combining solid research with good humor, Sapolsky explains how prolonged stress causes physical and mental afflictions. Chapters 2 and 4 describe the drain on biological resources.

3 Gary Austin is the founder and original director of The Groundlings, a well-known Los Angeles character-based improv company, which began in 1974. Learning improvisational acting from Gary taught me how to shift my emotions at will, especially under duress. He also taught me how to bring my whole self on the stage and off, in every conversation. His work was life-changing for me. I was sad to learn Gary passed away this year, yet I know many actors and teachers are living and sharing his legacy.

CHAPTER 4:   **REMOVING THE ROADBLOCKS**

[1] Tracy Goss was a pioneer in leadership transformation and organizational reinvention. She wrote *The Last Word on Power* to differentiate internal from superficial leadership powers to help identify sources of success when the tasks at hand look impossible to solve. The quote came from page 7 of the first edition of her book.

[2] Iyanla Vanzant wrote extensively about the need for willingness in her book, *One Day My Soul Just Opened Up.* Knowing what you need to do doesn't change behavior. Trying to convince yourself and others with facts can be a waste of time. The willingness to take the first step is needed to overcome fear and the attachment to anger and habits. The quote can be found on page 51.

[3] Joseph Campbell talks about the hero's journey in many of his books and lectures. He gives a wonderful account of how the journey relates to our own paths in the book compiled on a series of interviews with Bill Moyers, *The Power of Myth.* New York: Doubleday, 1988.

CHAPTER 5:   **MAKING POWERFUL CONNECTIONS**

[1] Julia Rozovsky, an analyst in Google People Operations, studied over 180 teams for two years at Google and wrote up her finding in a report titled, *What Makes a Good Team Effective?* She found that the mix of personality types, experiences, and positons didn't make the difference. "Who is on a team matters less than how the team members interact, structure their work, and view their contributions." Rozovsky identified the five keys to team success as: psychological safety, dependability, clarity on structure (goals, roles, and plans), the purpose of the work was

clear to everyone, and the impact of the results mattered. You can find the results at *https://rhttps://rework.withgoogle.com/blog/ five-keys-to-a-successful-google-team/*

2   Shunryu Suzuki, also known as Suzuki Roshi, said the mind of the beginner is needed to practice Zen. The ability to see things fresh and new can create expansion in all aspects of life. The empty mind is ready for possibilities, seeing new ways to interact and solve problems with ease. His book, *Zen Mind, Beginner's Mind,* is a wonderful treatise for joyful living.

CHAPTER 6:   INSPIRING GREATNESS

1   In *The Heart's Code,* Dr. Paul Pearsall documented work that points to the heart's power to align the body and mind, and to energetically connect with others.

2   The quote is from Amy Edmondson in her book, *Teaming to Innovate.* Jossey-Bass, 2013. There have been more recent books and articles written by Dr. Edmondson that explore the impact psychological safety has on creativity and innovation, but this is her foundational work.

3   In their study conducted through Case Western Reserve University, Richard Boyatzis and Ellen Van Oosten wrote their results in the article, *Developing emotionally intelligent organizations.* (2002) and published it in the book edited by Roderick Millar, *International Executive Development Programmes, 7th Edition.* London: Kogan Page Publishers, 2002. The paper can be found at *http://www.eiconsortium.org/reprints/ developing_emotionally_intelligent_organizations.html*

RESOURCES

Books

Allen, Steve. *How to Be Funny: Discovering the comic you.* Columbus, OH: Prometheus, 1998.

Bohm, David. *On Dialogue.* New York: Routledge Classics, 2004.

Buckingham, Marcus and Curt Coffman. *First, Break All the Rules: What the world's greatest managers do differently.* New York: Simon & Schuster, 1999.

Buber, Martin, trans. Walter Kaufmann. *I and Thou.* New York: Charles Scribner's Sons, 1970.

Campbell, Joseph, with Bill Moyers. *The Power of Myth.* New York: Doubleday, 1988.

Childre, Doc Lew, Howard Martin, and Donna Beech. *The HeartMath Solution: The HeartMath Institute's revolutionary program for engaging the power of the heart's intelligence.* New York: Harper Collins, 1999.

Csikszentmihalyi, Mihaly. *Flow: Psychology of Optimal Experience.* New York: Harper & Row, 1990.

Damasio, Antonio. *The Feeling of What Happens: Body and emotion in the making of consciousness.* New York: Harcourt, 1999.

Damasio, Antionio. *Looking for Spinoza: Joy, sorrow and the feeling brain.* New York, Harcourt, 2003.

Frankl, Victor. *Man's Search for Meaning.* Boston: Beacon Press, 1959.

Gazzaniga, Michael. Who's in Charge: Free Will and the Science of the Brain. Ecco, 2011.

Goleman, Daniel. *Emotional Intelligence.* New York: Bantam Books, 1995.

Goleman, Daniel, Richard Boyatzis, and Annie McKee. *Primal Leadership: Unleashing the Power of Emotional Intelligence.* Boston: Harvard Business School Press, 2013.

Goss, Tracy. *The Last Word on Power: Executive Re-Invention for Leaders Who Must Make the Impossible Happen.* New York, Currency Doubleday, 1996

Kahneman, Daniel, *Thinking, Fast and Slow.* Farrar, Straus and Giroux, 2011.

McKay, Matthew, Martha Davis, and Patrick Fanning. *Thoughts & Feelings: Taking control of your moods and your life.* Oakland, CA: New Harbinger, 1997.

Miller, Timothy. *How to Have What You Want: discovering the magic and grandeur of ordinary existence.* New York: Henry Holt, 1995.

Murphy, Michael, and Rhea A. White. *In the Zone: The transcendent experience in sports.* Reading, MA: Addison-Wesley, 1978.

Pearsall, Paul. *The Heart's Code.* New York: Broadway Books, 1998.

Pert, Candace. *Molecules of Emotion: The science behind mind-body medicine.* New York: Simon & Schuster, 1999.

Pink, Daniel. Drive: *The Surprising Truth About What Motivates Us.* Riverhead Books, 2011.

Ratey, John J. *A User's Guide to the Brain.* New York: Random House, 2001

Richardson, Cheryl. *Take Time for Your Life: A personal coach's 7-step program for creating the life you want.* New York: Broadway Books, 1998.

Rosenthal, Norman E. *The Emotional Revolution: How the new science of feelings can transform your life.* New York: Kensington Publishing, 2002.

Sapolsky, Robert M., *Why Zebras Don't Get Ulcers: The updated guide to stress, stress-related diseases, and coping.* W. H. Freeman and company, 1998.

Suzuki, Shunryu. *Zen Mind, Beginner's Mind.* New York, Weatherhill, 1990.

Vanzant, Iyanla. *One Day My Soul Just Opened Up: 40 days and 40 nights towards spiritual strength and personal growth.* New York: Simon & Schuster, 1998.

Whyte, David. *The Heart Aroused: Poetry and the preservation of the soul in corporate america.* New York: Doubleday, 1994.

Wilson, Edward O. Consilience: *The Unity of Knowledge.* New York: Vintage Books, 1996.

Zander, Benjamin and Rosamund Stone Zander. *The Art of Possibility: Transforming professional and personal life.* Boston: Harvard Business School Press, 2000.

Zukav, Gary. *The Seat of the Soul.* New York: Simon & Schuster, 1999.

Emotional Intelligence Coaching and Assessments:

Covisioning

Phoenix, AZ

(602) 954-9030

www.OutsmartYourBrain.com

Keynotes, Training, and Coaching:

Would you like to know more about how to outsmart your brain or do you know others who can benefit from what you learned in this book? Consider hiring Dr. Marcia Reynolds to deliver the keynote at your next conference, to provide an in-depth seminar for your organization, or to coach you personally to help you be more effective at work.

Marcia and her certified trainers offer speeches, one- to three-day seminars, executive coaching, and organizational development programs. She also provides customized coach training programs that can lead to professional certification by the International Coach Federation. For more information, call +1-602-954-9030 or read more and make your request online at *www.OutsmartYour Brain.com.* You can also email Dr. Reynolds directly at *Marcia@ OutsmartYourBrain.com.*

For additional articles, assessments, books, videos, podcasts, and training tools, go to *www.OutsmartYourBrain.com.*

ABOUT THE AUTHOR
Dr. Marcia Reynolds, PsyD

Dr. Marcia Reynolds is fascinated by the brain, especially what triggers feelings of connection, commitment, and possibility. This fascination led her to develop three areas of expertise: organizational change, coaching, and emotional intelligence. She draws on these areas as she helps leaders have more effective and meaningful conversations. When leaders have powerful conversations that respect the ideas of a diverse culture, the workplace comes alive with an eagerness to discover what is possible. She has coached and trained leaders in thirty six countries and has presented at the Harvard Kennedy School, Cornell University, Smith College, Almaty Management University, and Moscow School of Management at Skolkovo.

Marcia is a true pioneer in the coaching profession. She was the 5th global president of the International Coach Federation and is back on the Global Board. She is the Training Director for the Healthcare Coaching Institute at Virginia Tech and teaches at the International Coaching Academy in Moscow and for coaching schools in Shanghai and Beijing.

Prior to starting her own business, Marcia designed the employee development program for a global semiconductor manufacturing company facing bankruptcy. Within three years, the company turned around and became the #1 stock market success in 1993. The success was based on redesigning the organization into cross-functional business units to capture the brilliance and speed of diverse teams.

Interviews and excerpts from her books *Outsmart Your Brain, Wander Woman,* and her latest, *The Discomfort Zone: How Leaders Turn Difficult Conversations into Breakthroughs* have appeared in many places including *Fast Company,* the *Globe and Mail,* Forbes.com, CNN.com, *Psychology Today,* and the *Wall Street Journal,* and she has appeared in business magazines in Europe and Asia, and on ABC World News.

Marcia's doctoral degree is in organizational psychology. Her research emphasized the challenges and needs of high-achieving women in today's corporations. She continues to research what drives workplace behaviors, leadership effectiveness, and the science of motivation and engagement. She also holds two master's degrees in education and communications. Her website is *http://outsmartyourbrain.com/*

Other Books by Dr. Marcia Reynolds

The Discomfort Zone: How Leaders Turn Difficult Conversations into Breakthroughs, Berrett-Koehler, 2014.

Wander Woman: How High-Achieving Women Find Contentment and Direction, Berrett-Koehler, 2010

Made in the USA
Monee, IL
23 September 2022

14505491R00105